QA63 .O43 2018
3100100172792

Teaching Mathematics through Problem-Solving in K–12 Classrooms

Teaching Mathematics through Problem-Solving in K–12 Classrooms

Matthew Oldridge

ROWMAN & LITTLEFIELD
Lanham • Boulder • New York • London

Published by Rowman & Littlefield
An imprint of The Rowman & Littlefield Publishing Group, Inc.
4501 Forbes Boulevard, Suite 200, Lanham, Maryland 20706
www.rowman.com

Unit A, Whitacre Mews, 26-34 Stannary Street, London SE11 4AB

Copyright © 2018 by Matthew Oldridge
All figures created by author unless otherwise stated.

All rights reserved. No part of this book may be reproduced in any form or by any electronic or mechanical means, including information storage and retrieval systems, without written permission from the publisher, except by a reviewer who may quote passages in a review.

British Library Cataloguing in Publication Information Available

Library of Congress Cataloging-in-Publication Data

Names: Oldridge, Matthew, 1976- author.
Title: Teaching mathematics through problem-solving in K-12 classrooms / Matthew Oldridge.
Description: Lanham : Rowman & Littlefield, [2018] | Includes bibliographical references and index.
Identifiers: LCCN 2018021372 (print) | LCCN 2018039674 (ebook) | ISBN 9781475843347 (electronic) | ISBN 9781475843323 | ISBN 9781475843323 (cloth : alk. paper) | ISBN 9781475843330 (paper : alk. paper)
Subjects: LCSH: Problem solving—Study and teaching. | Mathematics—Study and teaching.
Classification: LCC QA63 (ebook) | LCC QA63 .O43 2018 (print) | DDC 510.71/2—dc23
LC record available at https://lccn.loc.gov/2018021372

∞ ™ The paper used in this publication meets the minimum requirements of American National Standard for Information Sciences Permanence of Paper for Printed Library Materials, ANSI/NISO Z39.48-1992.

Printed in the United States of America

For Nancy, my love, my best friend, and my partner in life, and for Callum and Alec—may you grow to see the beauty and wonder in mathematics.

Contents

Acknowledgments		ix
Introduction		xi
1	Toward a Definition of Teaching through Problem-Solving	1
2	What Do We Think about When We Think about Mathematics?	19
3	Ways of Thinking about and Representing Problems	33
4	The Mutually Complementary Nature of Procedural and Conceptual Understanding	47
5	Full Instructional Guidance and Deliberate Practice	61
6	Mathematics Classrooms Are Spaces for Talking, Reasoning, Thinking, and Wondering	77
7	Mathematics Can Be Playful	93
Coda: QED?		107
Bibliography		113
Index		115
About the Author		117

Acknowledgments

This work was greatly informed and shaped by many conversations over the years with friends and mathematics educators, particularly on Twitter. Thank you for being a part of the conversation and for not being afraid to "learn out loud" with me.

A few adapted ideas and thoughts from Melissa Dean, Melissa Pennarun, Jonathan So, Carol Mee, Jamie Mitchell, Sally Ghaemi, and James Cash are hiding in the text. Thank you for generously sharing your ideas.

Introduction

> There exists an elegant, interesting, and beautiful world of school mathematics, where students engage with interesting problems in their classrooms every single day.

Emily Dickinson had God in mind when she wrote, "He stuns you by degrees." I can honestly paraphrase her words and say, "Mathematics stuns me by degrees." Learning mathematics as an adult has given me access to a new world, one beyond space and time, a realm of the mind but one that happens to be uncannily good at explaining the physical world. Such is the raw power of mathematics as a way of thinking about and engaging with the world.

Spend some time thinking about the ladder that leads up to the tower of infinity, which leads up to the next tower of infinity, which maybe, possibly, leads to another tower, and so on and so forth, literally ad infinitum, and your logic, your very senses, your sense of the world, will be disrupted forever more. I want all our students, in all our classrooms, to be stunned by the beauty and magic of mathematics. I want them to see mathematics as a living and vibrant subject, something that is interesting to think about in its own right, outside of their school walls. Mathematics is a thinking tool, not just a subject in school.

As a newcomer to the poetry and beauty of mathematics but as a dedicated teacher and learner, I have often been stunned into submission, struck dumb by its raw power. Learning mathematics is humbling. I know a tiny slice of all the mathematics in the world, and I am but an elementary school teacher, but I want to know more and more. In knowing more, I want to teach more, to share with my students and fellow teachers interesting concepts and ideas from the world of mathematics.

I dream of a school mathematics where kids in classrooms around the world learn by engaging with interesting problems and talking about their unique and creative ideas for those problems. I dream of a school mathematics where interesting problems are the work itself and not just a side dish to be eaten after devouring many worksheets or a part-time distraction or a Friday reward for good behavior. I believe that we can teach and learn mathematics almost exclusively through interesting problems.

I have seen children blown away by their own unexpected insights. I have seen creativity and wonder flourish unexpectedly. Creative problem-solving and creative solution paths flourish in problem-solving mathematics classrooms. I have tried to make classrooms places of surprise and wonder. I have tried to make the physical spaces between the four cinder-block walls into wide open spaces for thinking.

"I wonder how many people have ever lived in the world?" kids have asked and then tried to come with the tools they need to model the answer. "Does pi ever end?" "What's the biggest number?" "What is infinity plus one?"

Our classrooms need to be these wide-open spaces for wondering and asking questions about mathematics, not just answering a potpourri of worksheet questions that curriculum documents have decided constitute "mathematics."

Problem-solving classrooms are places of guided discovery of massive mathematical ideas. We found pi because we needed to and wanted to, and you could do that, too, today with string and a ruler and a measuring tape and some can lids. We broke apart numbers, tore them apart into their atomic bits we call prime numbers, and put them back together again. We broke apart standard algorithms, as if looking under the hoods of cars, to see how they worked. We put them back together again, and then we played with numbers some more.

We play, we wonder, and we make conjectures about interesting topics in mathematics. We explain our thinking as we talk about our ideas. As humans, thinking is our birthright. We are born into an unceasing stream of consciousness, and we swim in it from birth until death. Consciousness is the biggest mystery, but it is a gift. We are capable of thinking about interesting and big mathematical ideas from a young age. As novice learners, we build our skill sets, our tool kits of operations and the skills and ideas we need to do mathematics, but we have time to play and, above all, to think along the way. Mathematics classrooms are places to think about big and open tasks and ideas and problems.

Jordan Ellenberg speaks of mathematics as extending our "common sense by other means." Teaching through problem-solving is helping our students to develop these "other means." Teaching through problem-solving is developing our intuition, enhancing our senses, and learning how to think using the tools of mathematics. It is visualizing, and it is bringing the objects of our visualization into being. Mathematics is an act of creation: if we can imagine it, then we can bring it into being.

Open the door of your classroom just a crack into the world of mathematical thinking and reasoning. Some kids will walk right through, and some, tentative and fearful, will want to stay behind. "Just give me a worksheet," they might say. Worksheets are sometimes preferable to thinking, or at least they are if we do not know any better. Now open the door a crack more—more kids will walk through. Now push the door of mathematical thinking open wide and expose all students to its power. Let them all walk right through that door forevermore.

We dream of a school mathematics that graduates students who are confident mathematical thinkers. We dream of a school mathematics that makes kids confident problem-solvers using the tools and ideas of mathematics.

It is my wish that no kids want to stay behind. The culture of "Where's my worksheet?" can change. What's behind the door of interesting problem-solving mathematics? Cold, hard logic, yes, and numbers, yes, but also shape, space, rates of change, quantity, graphs, chance, and many other things, only some of which are dreamed of in our curriculum (graph and category and game theory, obscure topological surfaces, non-Euclidean geometry, and many other things).

Behind that door is also play, that most human of desires, of modes and ways of being, and the thing we so desperately need in our mathematics classrooms. Mathematical objects are meant to be taken down from mental shelves—dusted, examined, and played with. Mathematics is not a museum full of relics and signs that say, "Look but don't touch," or "Only touch if you are a professional mathematician."

Francis Su, in his speech "Mathematics for Human Flourishing," convinces us that mathematics is, or could be, essential to human flourishing. He tells a story of a man who escapes the prison walls in which he is confined by teaching himself mathematics. He walks through a door in his mind and enters the mathematical world. It's a better one, a nicer one, and a more beautiful one than the world of the prison. There are no walls there, no locks, and no prison yard. He stays there, mentally free, until such time as he is physically free.

The backward E symbol in mathematics stands for "there exists" (see figure 0.1). It is used to bring into verbal being, into mathematical existence, either a unique object or a class of objects. I am thinking of one such unique object, which is found in classrooms worldwide. It is a school mathematics based on teaching through problem-solving. It is a school mathematics based on teaching through interesting problems that we can build together from simple axioms. It is a school mathematics that transcends the endless *Sputnik*-era political debate over "new math" and "old math." It is a school mathematics that blends skill practice and conceptual work so seamlessly we barely notice.

There exists a school mathematics that is beautiful, elegant, and true.

There exists a school mathematics that is rigorous and formal yet playful.

There exists a school mathematics where kids play with numbers, composing and decomposing with them, like a painter with paint or a master Lego builder with Legos.

There exists a school mathematics that builds a fundamental conception of arithmetic for kids from the fact that $1 + 1 = 2$. Counting is the basis of all arithmetic.

There exists a school mathematics where kids play with shape, space, arrangements, quantity, and chance.

There exists a school mathematics that coherently ties together big ideas of mathematics and is not a chopped salad of curriculum expectations or standards.

There Exists…

Figure 0.1. The backward E is used in mathematics to mean "there exists" when bringing an object or class of objects into being.

There exists a school mathematics that leaves all kids prepared for an increasingly data-driven and mathematical world.

There exists a school mathematics that combines cold, hard, steely-eyed utility with starry-eyed gazing on beauty.

There exists a school mathematics that leaves kids begging for more; going home at night to think about interesting tasks and problems; and coming back to school the next day with fresh energy, insights, and ideas.

This school mathematics could, and should, exist. But it doesn't. Instead we are tied up by politics, standardized testing, and fighting over ideologies and turf. We are bound by cycles of curriculum reform and periodic scares like *Sputnik*, which pit country against country in competition over who is best at mathematics, as if mathematics were a competition. We are tied up in words by op-eds on either side of the so-called math wars, where "back to basics" pedagogy is pitted as the mortal enemy of "new math," or "discovery," or "inquiry" math.

We fight about the meaning of school mathematics, and sometimes we change little things about how we teach mathematics, but we miss out on the full power of what could exist, of what we educators could bring into being together. Let's work together to bring this school mathematics into being. Beauty awaits. Elegance and insight await. Confidence and the power of unlocking students' own mathematical thinking awaits. We need to treat this as a matter of some urgency, so let's think it, write it, and talk it into being. Our students deserve no less.

There exists a school mathematics, where teachers teach through interesting problems and tasks, sparking fires of insight and curiosity in their students' minds. There exists a school mathematics. Let's work together to bring it into being.

Chapter One

Toward a Definition of Teaching through Problem-Solving

Axiom: Interesting problems are the mainstay of instruction in mathematics classrooms. Problem-solving is not a reward, special event, or a "once in a while" thing.

TEACHING THROUGH PROBLEM-SOLVING IS NOT "TEACHING PROBLEM-SOLVING"

Somewhere in the back of your classroom, on a dusty shelf, you might have an old binder full of problems. That binder might be organized by problem-solving strategies: working backward, solving a simpler problem, making a table or chart. If you wanted to teach your students about a certain strategy, then you chose a problem that goes with that strategy from the binder.

One such strategy is "working backward." The following is an example of the sort of problem typically used in older resources and textbooks to get students to "work backward" as a strategy for getting toward the goal of solving a problem:

> Jasmine and some of her friends collect comic books. Jasmine has twice as many comic books as JoAnne. JoAnne has two-thirds as many comics as Ava. Ava has 10 fewer comic books than Miriam, who has 31. How many comic books does Jasmine have?

Did you follow all that? With this problem, you can literally start with the last sentence and, like the strategy suggests, work backward. But is working backward the only strategy you would think to use? Maybe, just maybe, in the real world, you would each just count your own stack of comic books?

(Indeed, if you teach mathematics long enough, then you will encounter that kid who sarcastically answers, "Why don't we just count them?")

It was once deemed appropriate to teach students *about* problem-solving by teaching them to use specific problem-solving strategies to solve certain problems. Working backward, making a table or chart, and solving a simpler version of the problem are all strategies that we thought we could explicitly teach. Explicit teaching of problem-solving strategies would, the thinking went, help our students to grow as problem-solvers.

But problems in math classrooms should be taught in context of and in service of the mathematical content being worked on and studied. Teaching *about* problem-solving (problem-solving as a method) is worlds away from teaching *through* problem-solving (problem-solving as the main daily activity in the life of the classroom). In various curricula around the world, we find statements like we find in Ontario's mathematics curriculum: "Problem-solving forms the basis of effective mathematics programs and should be the mainstay of mathematical instruction " (Ontario Ministry of Education 2005; italics in original).

Since the 1980s, mathematics education has gone through several iterations of what might be called "problem-solving mania." As noted by Schoenfeld (1992), problem-solving was the "theme of the 80s" in mathematics education, with all interested stakeholders attempting to unravel and put into practice whatever this often-subjective term was deemed to mean.

Several more decades have since slipped by, and we are still debating how best to teach *through* problem-solving or, indeed, if that is even advisable. Debates over how best to teach any subject in any grade are never finished. Pedagogy is not settled science, and it is not something that can be subjected to rigorous proof, like mathematics itself. It is an art, and it is a craft, and as such, it is constantly revamped, revised, remixed, and improved.

Debatable as teaching methods are, we have learned that solving problems is not really something that can be taught through books full of categorized problems. Problems should not be sorted like they are vegetables. This "teaching about problems" or "teaching how to solve problems" approach has rightly fallen away. The school mathematics we envision is more fulsome and uses problems as the basis for exploring the mathematical ideas of the curriculum, building skills and understanding, and developing more flexible and capable mathematical thinkers.

As a child, perhaps you had a "problem of the week" to solve on Fridays. Engaging with a word problem was your reward for getting through four days of worksheets and assigned homework that was always taken up on the blackboard. You faithfully highlighted the key words in each problem (like you were taught) and went to work. Key words were signals to take action. You approached that problem as something mechanical to be taken apart in just the right way—preferably in that one way the teacher showed you—and summarized your work neatly in a sentence, being sure to include the "therefore" three-dot symbol.

Problem-solving as an event or reward is not what we have in mind for our school mathematics. It is not a cookie to be given after we have eaten our vegetables. It is not dessert. It is the main course itself—hearty and nutritious.

A DEFINITION OF *PROBLEM* FOR MATHEMATICS CLASSROOMS

> *Axiom: Problems are tasks or questions that are interesting and contain big mathematical ideas.*

What do we mean when we say "mathematics problems"? Any worthwhile mathematics task or question could be considered a problem. A problem is something that gets students thinking. A problem is not just a one-off question. A problem is a question but one that sparks more questions. A problem sparks more questions until the sparks make a raging fire of creative and mathematical thought. Mathematics is about question-asking as much as it is about question-answering.

Let our students be problem posers as well as problem-solvers. Let problems lead to more problems. A student's status in a mathematics classroom is typically that of a question-answerer. Problem sets are given, and students dutifully answer all of them. Students should ask as well as answer questions. If they are encouraged to develop their own questions, then they will come to see mathematics as a more generative and creative process of thinking and not just a process of answer getting.

To illustrate this idea, imagine you, teaching your typical unit about unit rates, ask students to relate a quantity of something to a measurement of one unit, whether that measurement is time, mass, volume, capacity, or something else. A textbook would typically give a series of exercises, perhaps designed to lead up to the consolidation of a specific calculation method, such as the cross-product. A typical context would be something like:

> 24 cans of dog food costs $8.99. At the same store, you can buy 10 cans for $3.99. Which is the better deal?

After working with a few examples of unit rates and thinking about where we find unit rates in our world, you could have students generate their own questions and contexts. In this way, you could create a class set of locally developed questions with contexts you know are meaningful because they have come from students themselves. You could open any grocery flyer or flyer app and come up with twenty questions using the basic structure of this one.

Try this with problems about the Pythagorean relationship. Textbooks and resources rely on the same tired contexts: ships at sea and ladders against walls. What if students created their own problems to practice applying the theorem? One student memorably created a problem involving the sight lines between Canadian pop star Justin Bieber and her in the audience based on the height of herself and the height of the stage. (Imagine he is shooting eye-beams from where he stands on stage, and those eye-beams are the hypotenuse of an imaginary triangle.) Creative and interesting problem variations abounded. Stale contexts were freshened and updated for our own classroom.

PROBLEMS INSPIRE THINKING

Problem-solving classrooms are alive with the sounds of students at work on mathematics that is big, wide, meaningful, and interesting to them. Problem-solving classrooms are where we go to think, not to avoid thinking. Let the students' thinking start slowly, but build to a crescendo, like the climax of a symphony or the loud part in a Nirvana song—a symphony of mathematics.

Problems are worthwhile mathematics tasks, and worthwhile mathematics tasks are those that get students thinking about big and important mathematical ideas. Problems, therefore, are task or question structures that get students thinking about mathematics that is interesting, useful, or beautiful. It is said that any piece of mathematics is worth doing if it is interesting, useful, or beautiful. Surely any question or problem you can assign, whether you found it in a textbook, online, or created yourself, can be made to fit at least one of these criteria. Mathematics is not an act of drudgery, like cleaning your garage (although even that would likely fit into the category of "useful," if you want to be able to find your things when you need them).

Create the interest. Find the beauty. Usefulness usually goes first, but you can leave it until later. The first two are the most important: create interest and find, if not beauty, at least *something* to admire in any problem, and students will stop asking, "When am I going to use this?" Consider two phrasings of this problem:

$$6 \times 1/2 = \underline{}$$

This is how a question about multiplying a whole number by a fraction might appear in a set of exercises, naked and alone. It is useful to know how to do this question if your teacher has assigned you this question and others like it.

You are unlikely to come across this expression, devoid of context, in the world outside the classroom. That context could be baking or construction or—cookies. There are lots of problems involving cookies in the world, especially if you spend any time around hungry children. Rephrase it as

Why is 6 × 1/2 equal to 3?

That is useful to know because the result is fewer wholes than you started with.

Try this more general formulation: *Why does multiplying a whole number by a fraction always make a smaller number? Can you give examples?* This more general version of the result is useful and perhaps interesting, especially if your students were expecting multiplication to make everything bigger, like they were taught early on in their mathematical training.

You could arguably find beauty in this simple expression, as well, by playing with different meanings of multiplication and seeing how they work—rotating a 6 by ½ rectangle to show the commutative property, for example, or showing how ½ is stretched 6 times on a number line to get to 3. This could be a good time talk about multipliers and multiplicands.

Beauty is where we find it and where we *create* it, and this expression could either be a part of a routine set of exercises or part of a series of problems posed about something bigger and wider, something that really makes us think. Humble and simple expressions like 6 × ½ are often taken for granted, but they are interesting as objects of thought in their own right.

PROBLEMS ARE THE OBJECTS OF THOUGHT IN PROBLEM-SOLVING CLASSROOMS

An old-fashioned definition of *problem* could be "any mathematics to be done," which would include any old worksheet full of endless exercises. We are picturing something a bit wider, broader than that. A definition of *problem* for our purposes is the following: "A problem is a mathematical question or task that is under consideration in a mathematics classroom." Problems are things we bring our mathematical tools, skills, and representations to bear on. You might have been expecting a more elaborate definition, but the parsimony principle of definitions insists on economy. "Under consideration" means "under thought." Thinking is a subjective and personal process, but problems are our objects of thought. We just need to learn how to think about problems. Some problems lend themselves to more interesting thoughts because they have more in them to think *about*.

Even the most seemingly routine worksheet can be problematic if we bring it to life. Even the most elaborate and intricate word problem can fall flat if we do not give it proper meaning. For many years, word problems have been the mountain summit of textbook sections—the point to which students climb to really show they know what they have learned after dutifully working the more routine examples along the way.

Many students give up before they reach the end, where the word problems are full of verbal trickery (and often too many words). There are thousands of problems in the world that have been given to students that are full of too many unnecessary words. These sorts of problems become exercises in reading comprehension; finding keywords; and, most of all, patience. They are not necessarily about mathematics or mathematical thinking. The problem with word problems is that they are often not interesting or problematic and contain too much extraneous information that must be filtered out. Here is one:

> Jagmeet wanted to help out his neighbor, who really likes fruit. He went to the store and bought 24 pieces of fruit. He purchased three times as many oranges as bananas. Jagmeet dropped by accident twice as many oranges as bananas, bruising them and causing them to need to be thrown out. He still managed to deliver 15 pieces of fruit to his neighbor. How many oranges were there?

The problem is designed to motivate the use of fractions, ratios, algebraic reasoning, or maybe just plain old arithmetic. It will probably just motivate a headache in the end. Just count the oranges, Jagmeet!

If they have worked through the routine exercises, the thinking goes, then students should be ready to transfer their knowledge. In many cases, these problems are hardly problematic at all, a bunch of numbers tossed into a forced context, like fruit tossed into a blender for a smoothie or fruit falling out of Jagmeet's hands, in the previous example. For all that these problems matter to our students, you may as well reach in, pull the numbers back out of the word problem blender, and have them make up their own problems with them.

"REAL-WORLD" VERSUS CONTEXT-FREE, OR "MATHEMATICAL-WORLD," PROBLEMS

"If Bobby has 3 apples and he gets 22 more and then 42 pumpkins and . . ." who cares. "Math has so many problems, why can't it solve them itself?" So goes the often-memed social-media statement. Math problems that get made fun of on social media are often about people buying large quantities of fruit for no apparent reason, usually cantaloupes or watermelons. You can't fool pragmatic Sally from Charles Schultz's *Peanuts*. Social media and the internet are where people go to poke fun at their own mathematical training and education.

Traditional word problems are frequently held up for mockery on the internet, and rightly so. Interesting mathematical ideas are often dressed up in boring or irrelevant contexts because they are presumed to be interesting to students. We commit a major fallacy here by assuming that mathematics itself is so boring that it must be dressed up, like broccoli smothered in rich, unhealthy cheese sauce when the broccoli flavor itself should be the star. It might be a learned taste, but it is nutritious and healthy (and, some might say, delicious).

There is a hierarchy of subjects in school. Art and physical education, for example, are often considered the "fun" classes. But for some of us, phys. ed. was a torturous ritual of volleyballs taken off the head and having circles run around us in soccer games. Art was scribbles on a page. In this hierarchy, poor mathematics is seen as more work than fun. This is another major fallacy. Mathematics is given a professorial reputation—stern, serious, a stuffed shirt at a lectern—when it could be holding court in the corner of the party, keeping others rapt with its interesting anecdotes and stories.

Mathematics teachers must have faith that mathematics is fundamentally interesting. Interesting problems do not necessarily need real-world contexts. It is assumed that real-world problems are always better because students are learning in the world, and there are interesting things in the world, and we must bring our academic work into their world. It is also assumed that, at some point, they will take their mathematical learning and apply it to the world, but when this happens, it is far more likely to be budgets or tax preparation or interest rates or the fractional size of screws they will use.

Teachers dutifully find and create problems that are in the real world because they have been told that real-world contexts are best for students. For example, buying a pair of sneakers could be the perfect motivation to get kids to do algebra. They could look up the price of Air Jordans and come up with a savings plan. They could model this plan with algebra because, of course, when kids want to save up for a $250 pair of sneakers, they always use algebra.

Wait! No, of course they don't. Students just take the amount saved per week and do some arithmetic. They compute until they get the answer they need. The context motivates simple arithmetic and not algebra, although it does make for a few interesting discussions along the way.

A few other common situations that are supposed to motivate the use of algebra: picking a plan from a cell-phone provider and maybe going bowling or to an amusement park. In the first case, cell-phone plans are generally "math proofed," so anyone going on company websites can read them and sign up without much math knowledge. The second and third cases are certainly in students' world but not really something they tend to think about algebraically. More likely, they have a certain amount of money to spend, and when they spend it, it's gone. "It's Saturday, so what are the fixed and variable costs of going to Six Flags today, and which equation would model that?" said no kid ever.

Students sniff out bad and phony numbers in word problems. Fake is fake, and it's hard to put one over on students. They are human nonsense detectors. Try giving them a problem that involves buying a video game for $15, when in the real world they are more like $60 or $80. That is an insult to their intelligence. You may as well take out an iPad or Chromebook, look up and compare a bunch of video game prices, and do some math from that. At least get current information. Better yet, make an inquiry out of it. Develop the problems from the information you find. You could ask a question like:

> How many video games could you buy for $150 dollars? Which ones?

With this problem formulation, students need to make purposeful choices based on their own research, apply sales tax, and calculate the price of various combinations from different stores. This could lead to more general and more critical questions like: Which store has the best deals? or Which video game system has the cheapest games?

Inquiry mathematics classrooms are classrooms where we find and use information and data to create mathematical models, make decisions based on our own thinking and modeling, and draw powerful conclusions. Problems lead to more problems, and questions lead to more questions, which students feel the need to answer. That is the inquiry cycle: question, answer, question, repeat.

We are used to living in *our* world, with all its familiar objects and things—the objects and things that we interact with and use in our day-to-day lives. These objects and things can indeed be turned into the stuff of mathematics problems, but we need to do that in authentic ways. We need to help our students to use mathematics to inquire about the world around them.

MATHEMATIZE YOUR WORLD

"Mathematize your lived existence" is a great mantra that teachers can use to think about problem creation, and it imagines us and our students looking around us and taking a mathematical viewpoint on common life situations, like shopping, playing sports, and walking around our home or school. We see the world with new eyes when we see it mathematically.

Many great tasks have been born from looking around and snapping photos in this age of ubiquitous mobile cameras. A picture of a Ferris wheel, for example, could be turned into a problem about circumference, which has more interesting visual information than that old black-and-white drawing in your textbook, and one that invites more thought. Many stellar unit-rate problems are born by snapping photos in grocery stores, where you compare the price by unit of several similar products. Discount signs are everywhere. Students can be taught to see their own very real world as mathematical.

We can mathematize our worlds, but the mathematical world *itself* is interesting enough sometimes. It is a world of logic and numbers and quantities and patterns. It is a world of pure thought, visualization, and eventually representation. Our classrooms should fuse the mathematical world and the real world. We know how to make our way in the real world; let us help students to access the mathematical world.

"Real-world problems" is a phrase that is thrown around with near recklessness, assuming, as we do, that engaging with the real world in math classrooms is always best. However, our students are sensitive to pseudocontext, as they should be. Problems about pizza or cookies are far too common and often not problematic enough. While you can get students to think about division as fair sharing easily by posing a cookie problem, you could probably also activate their thinking about that same idea in a more interesting way. Thinking about division itself is even more interesting than a forced problem about dividing cookies. What is division? How often do we think to start from just that question? Why is division the opposite of multiplication? Does *division* always mean "equal grouping"? Do two numbers, when divided, always make a smaller number? What do remainders mean? There is a whole book's worth of problems to be created from questions like these.

Forget broccoli. Sometimes we mathematics teachers treat our subject like parents treat cough medicine: something that will go down bitterly but is necessary for health and survival. It need not be that way. Likewise, we are not talking about pointlessly sweetening or watering down our subject matter. The mathematical world is an interesting place to be and to live. Our students need to be shown that mathematics can be a world, too.

Teachers make choices daily about which mathematics problems, questions, or tasks are worth engaging with. Our choices signal to students what we find interesting, useful, or perhaps even beautiful. Consider this:

> There is no other decision that teachers make that has a greater impact on students' opportunity to learn and on their perceptions about what mathematics is than the selection or creation of tasks with which the teacher engages the students in studying mathematics. (Lappan and Briars 1995, 138)

We have the power to shape the very idea of *mathematics* in the minds of our students through the tasks and problems we design, select, and use. Such is the power we wield when we design and structure our mathematics classrooms. Do we want students to think of mathematics as an endless procession of worksheets, homework to be dutifully completed, followed by unit tests of seemingly random items to check for understanding? Or do we want them to see mathematics as a vibrant, creative, living subject where we talk, think, conjecture, and wonder about interesting problems? The answer is hopefully clear.

A friend's daughter once said, "Math is numbers and annoyingness and hatred." Another student in sixth grade once said, "Math is the most powerful force in the universe." Other students think mathematics is fractions and multiplying and questions about cookies. Some just say, "Math is fun," and we want that—oh, how we want to hear that from our students. Conceptions of mathematics in students' minds can be quite rigid and fixed, even at a young age. Ask your students, "What is mathematics?" and see what they have to say. I revisit this question at the end of this book.

MATHEMATICS IS FULL OF "WILD THINGS," TOO

Hearing from working mathematicians about what their work is like is very instructive. Dr. Eugenia Cheng, a mathematician at the School of the Art Institute of Chicago, pianist, and author, speaks of how helpful a huge imagination is to mathematics. She should know: She works in higher-dimensional category theory, which deals with objects that very literally cannot exist in this world. Mathematics as an imaginative pursuit might seem counterintuitive to those of us who have experienced mathematics as a set of rules and procedures to be followed or a menu full of topics where the most recent "dish" was developed in the 1600s (calculus), and Mount Algebra is the top of the curriculum.

Consider for a minute the book *Where the Wild Things Are* by Maurice Sendak, where Max, confined to his room, brings a whole world into being. Max's imaginative world grows and expands to fill the entire page, through Sendak's artwork, as he travels across the sea to where the wild things live and then slowly shrinks again as the wild rumpus ends and he returns to his more mundane physical reality, in his bedroom, where he still has not eaten his dinner. Mathematics is full of "wild things," too—beasts too strange to be tamed and objects that we can barely imagine. We need all the imagination in the world to visualize and bring mathematics into being. Let the classroom rumpus begin! Let it be a voyage of discovery, a journey into the unknown. Unlike Max, we might never come back.

TOWARD A DEFINITION OF TEACHING THROUGH PROBLEM-SOLVING

Mathematicians love definitions. Precise definitions make mathematics possible but are also argued about, debated, and used in different ways. There was once created a one-hundred-page proof for "$1 + 1 = 2$." Mathematicians take nothing for granted.

There is certain subjectivity to teacher practice, where teachers are constantly refining and changing their practice over a career of thousands of school days. There is no single monolithic "best" pedagogy, but there exists "better" and "worse" pedagogies, and personal choices need to be made about how to teach, based on our beliefs, and our strengths and weaknesses as teacher-practitioners and as human beings. With already such a wide range of teacher practice, it is easy to get bogged down in competing or elaborate definitions.

This chapter defines *problem-solving* for our classrooms and creates axioms for teaching through problem-solving. These axioms are presumed to be true but are not necessarily axiomatic in a "true for all times and places" kind of way. They are necessarily informed by years and years of teacher practice; research; and, most importantly, working with and talking to students from kindergarten to high school.

Problem-solving in mathematics classrooms is something that all teachers of mathematics are familiar with, and yet it is relatively ill defined. Our stance toward problem-solving and our definition of it depend in large part on our beliefs about learning itself, our entrenched biases, and our years of experience at deploying pedagogical moves and designing instructional paths to help students learn. One could be said to teach in a more traditional way or a more progressive way. One might be informed by Dewey's twentieth-century theories or work, or one might hearken back to older, preconstructivist theories. Regardless of our personal pedagogical choices, we use problems to some extent in our mathematics classrooms, whether we define *problems* as "word problems" or as "routine sets of worked exercises." *Problem-solving* is a phrase that runs in the background for math teachers, like a hidden program on a computer, always present but perhaps not often activated and thought about. Let us work toward a definition of *teaching through problem-solving*.

Consider this definition of *problem-solving*: "The term 'problem solving' refers to mathematical tasks that have the potential to provide intellectual challenges for enhancing students' mathematical understanding and development" (Cai and Lester 2010, 1). Teaching through problem-solving means using problems, questions, or tasks that are challenging and invite mathematical thinking through both mathematical content and mathematical processes in our students. Problems are problematic, interesting, and objects of thought in mathematics classrooms. An interesting problem is an invitation "in" to a mathematical idea or topic or concept. It is a provocation that says, "Start thinking now."

A typical approach to teaching Pythagorean theorem, for example, might often start with putting "$a^2 + b^2 = c^2$" on the board and showing students how to work through a few examples. This is very explicit and deliberate instruction through worked examples, and it can be a powerful instructional method. However, it ignores perhaps two thousand years of geometric proofs and probably starts in the wrong place for most students: with algebraic abstraction. The Pythagorean theorem states something very specific about right-angled triangles and specifically about the relationship between their side lengths. It is fundamentally visual and best developed visually and geometrically. There are literally hundreds of visual and geometric proofs that have been developed over the years that could be used to spark thinking about this very specific relationship.

Let's consider a more open and broad approach to this topic. We could start by attaching squares to the sides of different triangles and seeing what we notice. In this instructional path, we are following in the path of the ancients and arriving at our own geometric proof. We are finding the Pythagorean relationship, as if for the first time.

Teachers lead their students on this journey, which is one of guided mathematical discovery. We don't need to "discover" old math to use it, but the thrill is in the sudden realization that there is "something happening here"; some specific relationship that we have noticed; something that we can see, touch, and eventually define and use. You have attached squares to right-angled triangles, and what have you noticed? One side always has a bigger square. Great! Now why is that? We can develop a visual anchor for the relationship before we pull out the mighty theorem and unlock its power by plugging numbers into the formula.

Try showing your students a picture of any television—let's say a fifty-inch TV. Televisions are sold by their diagonal length (the hypotenuse), as if the television was sliced into two right triangles. Could we show a picture of a television and invite conjectures about how long the length and height are? Many students feel there is some kind of trickery in selling televisions by the hypotenuse—the actual length is shorter than the hypotenuse. Unwary consumers may have forgotten or never learned the Pythagorean relationship or might not know this simple, useful fact.

Or, could we show one of those familiar shortcuts across the grass in a park, the worn path where people have chosen to cut across (the hypotenuse) rather than go around the outside? (Every park has a "Pythagorean shortcut." Go look—you'll see!) Open any dynamic mapping software or app, and look for some parks. You will find a worn Pythagorean path, perhaps in your neighborhood. This is the modern visual update to those old textbook problems about either walking along two edges of a parking lot to get where you are going or cutting across. Humans tend to cut across; either we have an innate sense of the Pythagorean relationship, or we just know shortcuts.

There is time in elementary and secondary classrooms to approach mathematics topics visually, and there is time to play with the concepts along the way. Concepts can be unlocked like achievements in video games through careful and patient work. Worked examples are important and necessary, but they can come later in the instructional sequence. Worked examples are generally more procedural than problematic; we want to invite students into the world of mathematical thinking by giving them problematic tasks.

Most old Pythagorean problems are trite examples of pseudocontext anyway. Ship traveling east and north, anyone? However, it is useful to know how to put a ladder against a wall in order to reach the height you want. Bring a ladder into the room, and slide it up and down the wall. How high up the wall can you get? Wieman and Arbaugh (2013) offer a useful definition of *problem-solving*: "by 'problems' in mathematics, we refer to mathematical tasks that are problematic" (11). Sure, you might say, but many things in the world are problematic: the behavior of celebrities and politicians, for example. Problems are problematic; water is wet. Fleshing out the word *problematic* might lead us to say things like, "Just giving kids formulas without developing them is not problematic," or "Questions that invite thinking are problematic." Perhaps by problematic we mean, resolvable after thinking about the problem and after applying the appropriate tools of mathematics.

Another phrase we commonly deploy in place of problems is *rich tasks*. A rich task could be said to be one that is engaging for students and contains a variety of entry points for all learners and interesting mathematical ideas. There are no rich tasks without rich classroom contexts, however. There are no teaching through problem-solving classrooms without teaching through problem-solving environments. Richness is found in classroom cultures themselves. Richness is not something that is inherent to questions in a resource. Teachers, as instructional designers, create classroom environments that make tasks rich: "Much of what it takes to make a rich task 'rich' is the environment in which it is presented, which includes the support and questioning that is used by the teacher and the roles the learners are encouraged to adopt. . . . [O]n its own a rich task is not rich—it is only what is made of it that allows it to fulfil its potential" (Piggott 2008). We make our tasks rich by having classroom environments that encourage and sustain mathematical talking, thinking, conjecturing, and wondering. In the right hands, even "8 × 7" can become a rich task because you could talk about

- different meanings of multiplication;
- the commutative property of multiplication;
- area models for multiplication;
- patterns in the times tables;
- known facts, near facts, and familiar facts; or
- the role of visualizing.

Problems can be problematic, and tasks can be rich. Have we reached a logical dead end in our search for a definition of teaching through problem-solving?

The following is a cautious, tentative definition of *teaching through problem-solving*, based on everything discussed so far: "Teaching through problem-solving is an instructional approach to mathematics that begins with a problem to be solved." It's by no means a full or complete definition, but it's a start.

PROBLEMS ARE THE VEHICLE FOR CURRICULUM

The late John Van de Walle (2004) comes in very strong with his opinion that mathematics should (must?) be taught through problem-solving: "It is important to understand that mathematics is to be taught through problem-solving. That is, problem-based tasks or activities are the vehicle by which the desired curriculum is developed. The learning is an outcome of the problem-solving process." The problems themselves are the very vehicle for the curriculum. They are no longer the broccoli on the side of the plate; they are the main dish. Ideas, skills, and concepts are developed by tackling interesting problems. The teacher's role is to deploy those problems, get out of the way for a while, and then to step in to help build conceptions or to dispel misconceptions. A period of (hopefully) productive struggle will occur, and after a certain length of time, students will enter the zone where the mathematical idea starts to reveal itself.

Rightly, this sounds a lot like "discovery learning." We are strong advocates for letting students explore concepts through interesting problems at the beginning of instruction about any given topic, but often we do not allow students to flounder, to struggle too hard and for too long, without explaining concepts to them when they need help. The key pedagogical move in teaching through problem-solving is knowing the amount of instructional guidance to give and when. It's not about letting kids "discover" ancient concepts; it's about making them *feel* like they discovered ancient concepts and helping them make sense of what they found. This powerful process of guiding students to understand mathematical concepts is a key feature of problem-solving classrooms.

In our model, a lot of the guidance we give comes at the end in the consolidation of the lesson. We are doing our students no favors if we leave them with incomplete or partial understandings at the end of a lesson or instructional sequence. It is not enough to just give problems for students to solve. A common complaint about constructivist approaches to teaching mathematics is that we do not give enough guidance, as minimal guidance is not enough to bring about learning in novice learners.

Kirschner, Sweller, and Clark (2006) address this in their article on unguided versus guided instruction: "Direct instructional guidance is defined as providing information that fully explains the concepts and procedures that students are required to learn as well as learning strategy support that is compatible with human cognitive architecture. Learning, in turn, is defined as a change in long-term memory" (75). The authors conclude that using worked examples and reducing cognitive load in our students is the best approach. Rather, there is an optimal amount of cognitive load that it is advisable to induce, but this amount varies from student to student.

But direct instruction on concepts and skills need not occur at the start of a lesson sequence. Teachers should not "give the game away" or take the mystery away by revealing the interesting mathematics of the lesson right at the beginning. Give kids interesting problems, let them play with them, and shape their thoughts and ideas about the important mathematical concepts at work while giving guidance along the way. This guidance could look like whole-group minilessons on key misunderstandings, small-group instruction for those with a specific misunderstanding, or individual feedback when needed.

There is a certain amount of time for struggle on a problem or task that is productive. The amount of time for which struggle is productive and not defeating or overwhelming varies from student to student and depends on their tolerance for ambiguity. There is a certain amount of ambiguity that can and should be tolerated in mathematics classrooms as we develop our understanding of ideas, topics, and concepts and learn to use procedures.

There is an interesting set of numbers called Frobenius numbers, where you take three numbers and determine the largest number that cannot be made with various combinations of those numbers. The Frobenius number of 6, 9, and 20, for example, has been called the "McNugget number," as 6, 9, and 20 correspond to package sizes. The McNugget number is 43, and there is a catch—a very big one: Every integer larger than 43 can be made with combinations of 6, 9, and 20. A colleague gave this problem to third-grade students and watched them struggle for more than an hour. You could not even say *struggle* because they were in the zone, that sweet spot of problem-solving where time seems to disappear. They were truly in the flow of problem-solving. We watched one student work out combination after combination, slowly, patiently, and faithfully. The problem and the scaffolding given by her teacher were just right, and so she persevered.

It is not about "throwing out the life preserver" too soon; let students find their own ways in interesting problems, let them struggle, and let them think. Knowing when and how to give instructional guidance is the important thing. A five-minute minilesson about a persistent or common misunderstanding is sometimes all that is needed. Conversely, you may find that some students get frustrated and angry. That is unproductive struggle, and we should intervene before they get to that point, providing the right advice, support, and help at the right time. Our problem-solving classrooms will oscillate between uncertainty and certainty, between ambiguity and proof. For the most part, we will live somewhere between these two poles.

Mathematics has a reputation for being a subject of cold, hard certainty, of proven truths and facts and of single right answers, but there is room for a lot of uncertainty along the way as we solve problems. Just ask Andrew Wiles, who thought about Fermat's last theorem since he was a child; later, as a professional mathematician, he worked for seven years on the theorem. He sometimes had to set his work aside because he reached unexpected dead ends. He probably wanted to give up, and at times the problem must have seemed, well, as unsolvable as it had been for more than three hundred years. Wiles needed to invent new mathematical tools to bring his ideas into being. He needed to connect ideas and areas of mathematics that had never been connected before. He obviously struggled along the way. He worked through his doubts. He made mistakes, and he fixed them. He published a proof and was told that his proof was wrong. He faced his errors and fixed his proof. Through careful, deliberate, and patient problem-solving, a door to the solution eventually opened, and he walked through it.

Fermat's last theorem was seemingly intractable, and Wiles's work is of towering significance. But we want the feeling he had when he broke through—on a smaller scale—for all our students in mathematics classrooms, from kindergarten to grade 12. Their problems are much smaller than anything faced by professional mathematicians, but they are still problematic to them. Our students must be taught to be as careful and patient in their own classes as Wiles was when working on his proof. We want them to be slow and patient thinkers, and we want them to be slow and patient problem-solvers. Slow down, and do mathematics. There is no rush.

Give an interesting problem to your class that is within their zone, something they have the mathematical tools to handle, and chances are there will be a sweet spot of problem-solving, maybe thirty to forty-five minutes in, where most students start to get it, where the structure of the problem is revealed and the answer starts to travel, as if by the power of thought, around the room.

Solution paths are created, and students walk down them. When students are in that zone, you hear the excited hum of math talk and the sharing of solutions. Mathematical ideas spread around the room, as if the X-Men's Professor Xavier is linking them by telepathy. Creative and interesting solutions start to appear. Problem-solving classrooms are wide-open spaces for talking and thinking about interesting problems.

The rest of this book focuses on developing the kinds of problem-solving classrooms we want for our students and that our students deserve. Thinking like mathematicians, let us try to develop some axioms for problem-solving classrooms. Axioms in mathematics are things that are generally regarded as self-evidently true and do not need to be proven, but let us approach these axioms in the following chapters with some skepticism and care.

AXIOMS FOR TEACHING THROUGH PROBLEM-SOLVING

1. There exists a school mathematics that is inspiring, interesting, playful, and elegant, where students work on challenging problems, together and alone, and share their own thoughts, ideas, conjectures, and reasoning.
2. Problems are tasks or questions which are interesting, and contain big mathematical ideas.
3. Interesting problems are the mainstay of instruction in mathematics classrooms. Problem-solving is not a reward, special event, or a "once in a while" thing.
4. All students can be taught to think mathematically.
5. Problem-solving is an iterative, ongoing process of thought.
6. Representation in mathematics classrooms is both a mental and physical activity—one of thinking about, and "bringing into being".
7. Basic skills and problem-solving (procedural and conceptual understanding) are not at odds, but rather are mutually complementary.
8. Full instructional guidance is a necessary condition of problem-solving classrooms.
9. Mathematics classrooms are places of talking, thinking, conjecturing, and wondering about the mystery and beauty of mathematics.
10. Mathematics can, and should, be full of curiosity, creativity, and play.

Chapter Two

What Do We Think about When We Think about Mathematics?

Axiom: All students can be taught to think mathematically.

What does it mean to think about mathematics? Are thinking about and *doing* mathematics the same thing? Does it even matter if they are or are not the same?

"Doing mathematics" can be considered as working on a mathematical object or problem or task and finding a way—with the tools of mathematics—to bring it into being in our world. Thought comes before action: thinking about mathematics must precede the doing of mathematics. Mathematical content itself is the vehicle for thinking mathematically. In mathematics classrooms, teachers create or find that content and give it to students. But what does it mean to "think mathematically"?

Years ago, I titled my first teacher blog *Open Spaces for Mathematical Thinking* and put forth my tentative, early ideas about mathematics teaching and learning. I wanted to create a big, wide-open space within the four walls I worked. I wanted to create an endless mental plane or zone for thinking, for wondering, for speaking aloud about mathematical ideas. To create this space, I needed to get my students to forget about how they had thought about mathematics before. Some—accustomed to answer giving, worksheets, and tests—resisted. Stubbornly and steadily building an open classroom culture based on interesting problems gradually won most students over.

Our students can be taught to think mathematically, which entails stripping problems down to their essentials and taking action by representing those problems in the physical world with concrete objects, manipulatives, models, figures, representations drawn on paper, or spoken or written words. Enacting mental representations with words, diagrams, and representational tools is a goal of mathematics instruction in problem-solving classrooms. Our students can be taught how to think about mathematics and how to bring their thinking into being in their classrooms.

Problem-solving classrooms are concerned with this process of "bringing into being." Problem-solving classrooms create something from nothing. Problem-solving classrooms make tangible and visible what was intangible and invisible before. Problem-solving classrooms connect thoughts to actions, with teachers bridging the divide between the novice and the experienced by giving students opportunities to think about interesting mathematics and helping them to make sense of their thoughts.

We have perhaps not always or not explicitly thought of our mathematics classrooms as thinking classrooms. Peter Liljedahl (2015) defines a "thinking classroom" as a "classroom that is not only conducive to thinking but also occasions thinking, a space that is inhabited by thinking individuals as well as individuals thinking collectively, learning together, and constructing knowledge and understanding through activity and discussion." It is possible to make mathematics classrooms places of routinization, near automation, which Liljedahl might call "nonthinking classrooms." Reflect on your own mathematics education. Did you mostly sit in thinking or nonthinking mathematics classrooms?

A thinking classroom is a thinking space—a physical space for learning and a mental space that is open for work on interesting problems. Problems themselves are no guarantee of thinking, and other teacher choices matter very much: how to structure mathematical conversations, how to record student work, and the daily culture of the classroom.

MATHEMATICS IS WORTHY OF AESTHETIC CONSIDERATION

Automation and routinization are the enemies of thinking. This was true in the industrial age, and it is perhaps even truer as we enter the artificial intelligence age. Technological change is constant, but humans persist, and we are thinking beings. We have outsourced many routine and mundane tasks of life to machines, and more and more routine tasks will continue to be given to computers. Machines can apply cold, hard logic, for logic is what they are programmed to use, but thinking is still the human advantage. Classrooms are no place for automation. Teaching and learning is a human act.

We are perhaps more used to considering poems, paintings, and novels as objects of our thoughts than mathematics, for example. Artistic objects are endlessly interpretable, with no single closed or final interpretation. It is understood that works of art are meant to be thought about deeply and for long periods of time, until they reveal their structure, depth, and beauty to us, the beholders. This is our aesthetic impulse—we seek beauty around us, and we appreciate it when we find it.

Examining a work of art for a long enough period of time brings about a certain gestalt in beholders' minds, a fullness of interpretation, a bringing into being of an interpretation about the artwork itself. Kandinsky, with his own artistic language of point, line, shape, and plane, created geometric worlds in his art. Our understanding of his work is enhanced if we know his geometric philosophy. American artist Mark Rothko, with his wide swaths of color in many layers, presents seemingly simple canvases that also open up the longer we consider or gaze on them. From simplicity, depth is created. Various shades and hues of colors are mixed and wash over his canvases, creating depth that is not apparent on first viewing.

Poems are aesthetic objects that can be stripped down into their component lines, images, and unique word choices. Meter may or not be present. Rhythm and rhyme may or may not be used. Line breaks are chosen purposefully for meaning and effect. Startling and striking images are used uniquely. Words are endlessly interpretable, and poets from Shakespeare to Emily Dickinson to Bob Dylan are the subject of essays and interpretation over the centuries. Words are mysterious, and words are magical. They are obviously worthy of aesthetic consideration.

Our aesthetic senses are strongly at play when we behold artwork or read poetry, whereas mathematics—or at least school mathematics—is thought of as more utilitarian or mechanical. Professional mathematicians have favorite theorems, ideas, or proofs in which they find the same aesthetic beauty that others find in artworks: Euler's theorem or Cantor's diagonal proof of infinite sets. Professional mathematicians can look on a piece of mathematics and say precisely why it is beautiful.

The late Hungarian mathematician Paul Erdos considered particularly lovely or beautiful proofs as being part of *The Book*, a kind of holy text full of perfect mathematics. Others might have a favorite theorem or piece of mathematics, something that appeals to their own unique sensibilities. Indeed, there is a podcast called *My Favorite Theorem*, where mathematicians explain why they love particular theorems. Their aesthetic senses, finely honed through years of training, have led them to appreciate mathematics as rigorous, logical, and artful.

Mathematics itself is as worthy an object of aesthetic thought as art, and all students can be taught to find the beauty in mathematics. The aesthetic impulse is the thinking impulse, and thinking mathematics classrooms capture mathematical objects—the "things" of mathematics—as objects of thought in words or writing. Advanced mathematical structures will remain hidden to students. I am not talking about tackling category theory, advanced algebraic topology, the Riemann hypothesis, or the Goldbach conjecture here. Rather, I am talking about finding beauty as our students travel along the continuum from beginner to novice to more experienced thinkers about mathematics.

There is loveliness to be found along the way, for example, as students range over the number landscape, from birth to learning to count to developing operation sense through addition and subtraction, all the way through to working with more advanced operations. Students zig and zag all over this landscape as they learn, hopefully taking time to admire the scenery. There is no one set path, but there are opportunities to slow down and appreciate the view.

LEARNING TO THINK AND LEARNING TO THINK MATHEMATICALLY

It is obvious that thinking is our birthright as humans, but slightly less obvious is that mathematical thinking is also our birthright. We are given the mysterious thing called consciousness as we are born, and for the most part, we use our consciousness wisely. We need to use it wisely and well in service of mathematics. Thinking is one of the things we humans do best—most of the time. A world where we all use our ability to think about and use mathematics is a world we want for our students. We humans are born into an unceasing and unending stream of conscious thought, and we swim in that stream of consciousness from birth until death. Thoughts come along the stream, like fish, through synaptic connections, and we harness them, use them, and let them lead us to action. Mathematical thoughts also pass by like fish in this stream, and our students can be taught to fish for them.

While they are not mathematicians, our students are novices at *thinking mathematically*. Thinking mathematically is, therefore, not something that is esoteric or obscure or the domain of professional mathematicians. Thinking mathematically is something we can all train ourselves to do. The best way to learn to think mathematically is to do lots of mathematics and to pay attention to what you thought about while you did mathematics. It is teachers, as more experienced thinkers and instructional designers, who give interesting problems and contexts, and it is teachers who help students to slow down and become aware of, attend to, and monitor their own mathematical thinking processes.

Our ability to train ourselves to think mathematically is probably something that distinguishes us from most animals, creatures of pure instinct that they are. Some animals have rudimentary mathematics or at least the concept of "one, two, many" or the ability to instinctively account for their children. But we humans have learned to count, and we have learned to harness the power of counting into more powerful operations, like addition and multiplication. We have developed the abstract symbol system and way of thinking we call mathematics, and with training, we are well equipped to use it.

Students should see mathematics as a powerful way of thinking to engage with the world around them. Our students should finish their schooling knowing that mathematics is a thinking tool and not just a subject they leave behind when they are done with school. School mathematics courses should teach students to engage with the world around them using the tools of mathematics.

In school mathematics, our students should produce powerful representations of interesting mathematics by thinking about interesting mathematics. They bring the mathematical objects of their thought into the world, through their spoken words and explanations and on paper. Students learn, for example, what a fraction is; how to represent fractions with concrete objects, manipulatives, and models; and how they know their representations are accurate and true. They cannot represent a fraction without thinking about that fraction. A fraction is more than just a numerator and a denominator, which is the notation we happen to use to show fractions abstractly as numbers. Students must be taught to represent fractions in various ways before they can work with fractions symbolically. Representations themselves are both the products of mathematical thought and their representation in the classroom, as is shown in the next chapter.

Mathematics does not belong to schools, although school is where most of us do the most mathematics, unless we grow up to be mathematicians or work in a mathematics-related field like computer science, statistics, finance, or engineering. We don't just leave mathematics behind when we walk out the school doors for the last time, though.

As mentioned earlier, Jordan Ellenberg (2014) says that, when you are doing mathematics, you are "extending your common sense, by other means." An "otherness" implies a certain unnaturalness to doing mathematics, but it should not and need not be that way. Mathematics is not "other" to the human experience. Mathematics is *part* of what makes us human, and common sense is for life.

FEAR AND LOATHING OR LOVE AND APPRECIATION?

If you take a Platonic view, you may see mathematics as something otherworldly, a perfect and celestial object that casts a shadow on the world we see. It could be seen as existing objectively and independently beyond human experience, out there somewhere for us to find. Or, it is something that is created by humans through language and culture, a body of knowledge developed over time. Both viewpoints have merit, but teaching and learning are fundamentally human acts, and in our classrooms, mathematics is intertwined with human consciousness and the lived experience of our community of learners. Our students can be taught to access the mathematical world as a powerful extension of their more ordinary, everyday senses. They can be trained to develop these "other means," which means finding new and mathematical ways to perceive the world around us.

We consider the process of acquiring literacy as natural for our children because we are immersed in print, the abstract symbol system we call letters and words, in the environment all around us from birth. Letters and words are just the tools of literacy development to be gathered and used. Numbers—our abstract symbol system that allows us to be more specific than just "one and more" or "a few" or "a group of things"—are also ubiquitous in our world. Spend enough time around a three-year-old, and you are likely to hear spontaneous renditions of the rote counting sequence. Numbers appear on signs and in stores and in books in young children's worlds. Parents and teachers should treat number acquisition as naturally as language acquisition. Problem-solving classrooms seek to naturalize, as much as is possible, the process of mathematical development.

For far too long, a culture of fear of and even outright hostility toward mathematics has persisted. When did it become culturally acceptable to say, "I was never any good at mathematics?" When faced with the prospect of doing mathematics, many otherwise-competent adults throw up their hands and say, like Melville's Bartleby, "I would prefer not to." Numeracy (using mathematics in our lives), like literacy, is empowering, and our students will become adults who adopt attitudes of either fear and loathing or love and appreciation of mathematics.

NUMBERS AS OBJECTS OF MATHEMATICAL THOUGHT

Numbers are mathematical objects that we can develop new ways of thinking about. Numbers are far more than just sets of things we chant in a rote sequence over and over as small children, until we can say them by heart. Likewise, numbers are far more than just objects to be put into times tables, where we dutifully spit out the answer to phrases like "9×7," and "8×6" at the demand of a teacher and a timer. Numbers themselves are inherently interesting. Our students can be taught to play with them, to strip them down into their essential atomic prime units, to seek patterns, and to find their own personalities and characteristics. Maybe you have a favorite number. Maybe a number speaks to you, like "lucky 7" or "4" (inauspicious in China) or "23" (Michael Jordan or LeBron James, depending on your age). Maybe it's your house number as a child or your phone number. (Me, I think 111 is interesting, only because it seems like it should be prime but it is actually composed of 37×3.)

Our students should see numbers as things to play with, or even toy with, like cats do with mice. We do not all need to be like the great Indian mathematician Ramanujan, who had a close and seemingly intimate relationship with many numbers and saw perfection in seemingly strange numbers like 1,729 (the smallest number that can be expressed two ways as the product of cubes). We can all enjoy numbers and appreciate their unique personalities. We can enjoy stripping numbers down to their essential core bits, which we call prime factors. We can play with number lines and hundreds charts, discovering new patterns and relationships as we go. We can find beauty in highly composite numbers, like 24, or in strange primes, like 41, or even in numbers that seem like they should be prime, like 91 (13 × 7). All students can learn to do even larger multiplication products in their head, like 12 × 25. We can develop our mental machinery for computation and our spatial and reasoning sense about number itself. Consider this calculation:

> What do you think about when you think about two-digit-by-two-digit multiplication? How do you do it in your head?
>
> $$51 \times 25$$

Do not tell me you can't do it in your head. What do you see? What do you think about? If your first thought is to take out a pencil and paper or your phone's calculator, then slow your thinking down.

Now consider this problem, which was famously given to an eight-year-old Gauss:

> Pay attention to your thinking as you solve this problem. What do you do to break this problem down to make it easier for you to solve? What patterns do you find?
>
> What is the total of the whole numbers from 1 to 100?

How can we possibly calculate this total without turning to a calculator? How would you, as an educated adult, approach this problem? What tools would you use to find an answer? How would you even start? What representations or tools will serve you in attacking this problem? Do you have any mental imagery that appears in your mind when you think about this problem? What operation do you think will help you get a result?

If you have considered these questions, then you have experienced what it is like to be a mathematical thinker. You and your students will either step up to or shrink from this problem. A problem-solving mind-set is necessary here. A "strip it down to its essentials and find what is there" mind-set is necessary here. A mathematical thinking mind-set is necessary here. The object of our thought is the very familiar operation we call addition. Traditionally, students might be taught that the word *total* in a math problem is a signal to add together the numbers that are in the problem. (Indeed, you may have been asked exactly that by one of your students: "Does *total* mean 'adding'?")

Students are taught that keywords signal specific action or actions that they should take to *get the answer*. In a classroom approach that teaches *about* problems, keywords spark the doing of mathematics within the narrow of range of what is signified by the keyword. Students who are problem-solvers and not just answer getters will be more confident and comfortable along the way.

In problem-solving classrooms, we picture something a little broader and more open. Problems themselves are the objects of thought in problem-solving classrooms, and problems must be thought about to solve them. Keyword or rigid problem-solving approaches can impede thought. Keywords are handy shortcuts, and *total* will always signify addition, unless, of course, we recognize that summing a whole bunch of numbers together is much easier if we use multiplication.

A novice problem-solver tends to apply brute force to this problem, starting with 1 and beginning to add, either on paper or with a calculator. At some point, we hope they realize that there is a faster and perhaps better way. Seeking efficiencies is part of thinking mathematically. You might realize that you can use multiplication as a shortcut, or you might realize, as some students do, that you can come up with a general formula to calculate this sum. We hope our students will start to see shortcuts and patterns and begin to clump the numbers together to find a shorter solution path.

Our students might not recognize it at the time, but their primary education is a process of "powering up" from learning to count to learning to add to learning to multiply. They then add stronger and more diverse tools, like roots, exponents, and factorials. They also progress generally from being in a condition of pattern recognition of recognizing two repeating elements in kindergarten (e.g., an AB pattern) to being able to find relatively complex algebraic relationships by the end of high school (e.g., quadratic equations). If we just give this problem as it is, our students may or may not be able to find way to solve the problem. Given a problem that is unfamiliar, students often freeze in the moment, unable to find a door to open. Maybe there are simply too many numbers in the problem. Consider what might happen if you scaffold their learning by giving a hundreds chart immediately upon starting this problem (see figure 2.1).

Giving a context-free and unfamiliar problem like this one to novice mathematical thinkers induces a certain amount of cognitive load; teachers

1	2	3	4	5	6	7	8	9	10
11	12	13	14	15	16	17	18	19	20
21	22	23	24	25	26	27	28	29	30
31	32	33	34	35	36	37	38	39	40
41	42	43	44	45	46	47	48	49	50
51	52	53	54	55	56	57	58	59	60
61	62	63	64	65	66	67	68	69	70
71	72	73	74	75	76	77	78	79	80
81	82	83	84	85	86	87	88	89	90
91	92	93	94	95	96	97	98	99	100

Figure 2.1. A hundred square is a useful thinking tool to access problems. Do you see any patterns that can help you total all these numbers?

need to find the optimal amount of cognitive load to give, neither overwhelming nor underwhelming their students. Teachers are familiar with that puzzled look that students have when they begin to work on a problem. Some never find a way in. Some are afraid to start because they are scared of being wrong. Some give up in frustration immediately, conditioned to be intimidated by word problems or new mathematical situations. Some students never come to see themselves as mathematical thinkers with their own range of tools and strategies they need to attack problems.

Thinking tools and models such as the hundreds square help our students to build a line of attack on a problem. A student with a hundreds chart might notice that you can total row by row or column by column to reduce the amount of work. They might see different ways of grouping to reduce their workload. The total of 1 to 10, for example, is 55. Some students, after totaling the first row, will multiply by 10. This is too quick a generalization to make. It seems reasonable but leads to a false result. A course correction is needed: "Why is the total of the second row much bigger than the first row?"

We would not expect young kids to get to the algebraic formula for the sum of natural numbers that a very young Carl Friedrich Gauss found, but we should expect them to find patterns like the one Gauss found. He matched 1 and 100, to make 101, then matched 2 and 99, and so on. Try this yourself by looking at the hundreds chart. Gauss realized that he needed to multiply the 50 pairs by 101 to get 5,050. We are novices, not mathematicians, but neither was Gauss as a child. He was only eight years old, so the story goes. With very young students, you could develop a context that requires them to calculate the total of 1 to 10. Our young students could use physical counting objects to represent their thinking and to find patterns. With slightly older students, you could chop the problem in half: Total the numbers from 1 to 50. With higher grades, you may want to issue the following challenge or extension:

> Can you total the numbers to 1,000? How does knowing the total of 1 to 100 help?

For seventh- or eighth-graders, we could guide them toward the algebraic structure for the sum of natural numbers, even if the exact formula is out of reach. Consider whether your students are ready to have the curtain pulled back to see the formula for sum of a series of natural numbers:

$$\frac{n(n+1)}{2}$$

If they are, then great. Go there. They have unlocked a powerful generalization. Have them plug in a very large value for n and see what comes out. If not, sequence the sharing of the student work such that you can look at the diversity of approaches to the problem. Students are inspired by others' thinking, and problem-solving classrooms are open spaces for sharing our thinking. Gentle teacher guidance is necessary to push our students' thinking. As novice mathematical thinkers, they benefit from exposure to a wide range of thinking about problems and guidance toward more advanced or efficient methods.

DEFINING MATHEMATICAL THINKING FOR KINDERGARTEN TO GRADE 12 CLASSROOMS

Mathematical thinkers are confident in new situations, knowing that they are capable of solving any problem. Mathematical thinkers know that the process of solving a problem is often just as important as finding the answer. In teacher professional resources, the definition of *mathematical thinking* is often slippery and ill defined, if not avoided outright. In the world of working mathematicians, it has a wide variety of definitions. For K–12 classrooms, in Keith Devlin's (2012) words, "Mathematical thinking is a whole way of looking at things, of stripping them down to their numerical, structural, or logical essentials, and of analyzing the underlying patterns. Moreover, it involves *adopting the identity* of a mathematical thinker." In this approach, our students become confident in their identities as growing mathematical thinkers and are ready and able to use their skills and tools on any problem, provided it is within a reasonable range of difficulty. They will not look on any new situation with fear but rather with curiosity. They will pick and pull apart classroom tasks and problems until they can find their essential core, the fundamental and interesting mathematics at play in them.

Paul Lockhart (2002) describes mathematical thinking as the

> art of explanation. It's about actively developing deeper knowledge, understanding, and awareness of mathematical concepts, practices, and processes—more specifically, *analyzing how, evaluating why,* and *creating new ways of thinking about and using mathematics.* It focuses on deeper understanding of procedural knowledge, deeper thinking about conceptual knowledge, and deeper awareness of how mathematics can address, handle, settle, or solve real world issues, problems, and situations.

Both Devlin and Lockhart provide good descriptions of mathematical thinking. In problem-solving classrooms, we are stripping tasks, problems, and questions down to their essentials, considering which important mathematics are present in them, deciding which tools we need to bring to bear on them, and creating solutions to those problems.

This is not to say that all students will generate unique and inspired work; many problems end up circumscribed by a very narrow range of strategies and types of solutions. It is, however, to say that each student will use their own idiosyncratic thinking processes to engage with, think about, and solve mathematical problems. Our students need to be known and valued as unique and powerful mathematical thinkers. Most importantly, our students as young mathematical thinkers will be motivated to find their way along the solution path.

For kindergarten to grade 12 classroom purposes, the following is a proposed definition of mathematical thinking: *Thinking about and analyzing mathematics tasks, problems, or questions; finding their essential elements; bringing appropriate mathematical tools to bear on them; and verbally and visually representing your thoughts in the form of solutions.* Thought without action is not useful in classrooms, where teachers must assess and grade their students. Thoughts are fleeting, and thought processes are transient and difficult to verbalize. Mathematical representations exist as the result of thought. Mathematical thinking without an end result of representation is perhaps not mathematical thinking at all. Novices must be taught to build their own powerful mental apparatus of mathematical thought. What do they *see*, in their mind's eye, when they approach a problem?

All of this is not to say that novices (students) always think like experts (mathematicians). School mathematics and professional mathematics are not the same thing. There is a vast gap in skill, practice, expertise, and the recognition of various problem types. The more mathematics you do, the more strategies and tools you will have at your disposal. The more problems you do, the better you will be at solving problems. If there is a certain circularity to this reasoning, it is necessarily so. The best way to get better at doing mathematics is to do more mathematics. It is the teacher's job to make concrete, explicit, and visible the process of thinking that goes into solving problems.

A kindergarten student has a very small formal repertoire for attacking problems. Let's imagine they have a little toolbox with a few select things in it: numbers in sequence, sets of objects (once they have an established sense of cardinality), and maybe a limited sense of things like "2 + 2 = 4." Tools for attacking and working on problems are limited in our novice learners and, in younger grades, consist mostly of applying basic operations, creating visual pictures or diagrams, or representing their thinking with physical manipulatives. As students pass through the grades, they add more and more "things" to their mathematical tool kits.

Problem-solving is domain specific, meaning problems have specific mathematical content, and we need to open our tool kits and take out the tools we need to work on certain problems, just like a mechanic opens up her toolbox to work on your car. You don't use a hammer when you need a screwdriver, but you need to have been in enough situations that require hammers or screwdrivers to know the difference.

Students are still capable of complex and interesting mathematical thinking as novices, but it is our job as teachers to guide them further in their development. Teachers guide by helping to unpack word choices in problems and helping students to develop and work with visual tools and models, like open number lines, hundreds squares, counting objects, arrays, the area model, and the powerful tools for efficiency and speed that we call algorithms.

Students can adopt the identities of (young) mathematicians in the same way that they can adopt the identities of (young) scientists: by using some of the tools of the disciplines as they work at their own level and as they work through building their mathematical tool kits and their understanding of mathematical concepts. Students of all ages are encouraged to construct scientific hypotheses about the world and to test them, whereas it is far too easy for us to present all school math as axiomatic, prescriptive, programmatic, or universal without giving students a chance to see into the mathematical world themselves. In other words, if we present mathematics as a series of rules, procedures, and algorithms to follow, then we are depriving our students of the chance to think.

Consider a situation where a student has been taught through rules, procedures, and algorithms from grades 1 to 8. This student, by the time she reaches grade 9, will be uncomfortable and even visibly distraught at the idea of tackling novel problems. You may have met this student before. She does not see herself as a capable and confident mathematical thinker. She has not adopted the identity of a problem-solver, and more importantly, she has not adopted the identity of a mathematical thinker. A state of learned helplessness sets in over the years for these students, and mathematics becomes just another subject to "get through." We want more for our students.

Novice mathematical thinkers are still, in Devlin's definition and ours, stripping problems down to their fundamental elements. They are still, as Lockhart would have it, practicing the art of explanation. They are still interpreting problems and coming up with representational tools and deciding which operations or procedures to bring to bear. They are not working on the twin prime conjecture or advanced problems in algebraic topology, but they are still working on problems. They are not working on the unsolved million-dollar millennium problems, but they are learning how to approach problems as vehicles for developing their own mathematical skills and for knowing mathematical content itself. Learning how to start when faced with any mathematical problem or task is the hardest part.

Keeping the expert–novice divide in mind, then, the following are some things that professional mathematicians do that students generally do not do:

- construct formal proofs using rigorous logic and syntax
- use advanced notation to construct an argument
- develop theorems

But there are many things that both professional mathematicians and students should do.

> The thinking of professional mathematicians and K–12 students is alike when students
>
> - convince themselves and others of the truth of their solutions;
> - make and explore conjectures;
> - explore fundamental truths about arithmetic, like the commutative, distributive, or associative properties;
> - systematically attempt to find why something is true for all cases (e.g., why the formula for the area of a triangle works for all triangles);

- deploy formulae or algorithms after first exploring why and how they work;
- make generalizations using algebra (e.g., about a particular linear pattern);
- choose the best mathematical tool for the job, whether addition, subtraction, multiplication, division, or higher-powered and more sophisticated tools;
- use visual thinking tools and models, like arrays, open and closed number lines, and the area model, to visualize problems;
- create representations in the form of pictures or diagrams with mathematical content to solve problems;
- construct models for how things might work in the context of a given problem;
- know that analyzing problems takes just as long, and often longer, than arriving at a final solution;
- are comfortable with ambiguity during the problem-solving process;
- are prepared to change course if a problem-solving technique or path is not working.

In this list of actions, we find things that all students can and should be doing while learning in problem-solving classrooms to grow as mathematical thinkers.

Chapter Three

Ways of Thinking about and Representing Problems

Axiom: Problem-solving is an iterative, ongoing process of thought.

Georg Polya's *How to Solve It*, originally published in the 1940s, was his attempt to create a method for his university students to solve problems in mathematics. Polya sought to give his students generalized ways of thinking about mathematics problems to allow them to start, strategize, and monitor their own thinking when solving any problem. *How to Solve It* is a book-length heuristic for mathematical problem-solving, where a heuristic is a shortcut mental strategy. We use heuristics all the time in various avenues of our lives; we just tend not to think about them (indeed, they are often things that help us to avoid thinking).

They are guidelines, rules of thumb, or ways of approaching various situations and problems in our lives. They are practical strategies that we, often unaware, use to structure our lives and to make our way in the world. Polya sought to develop a way of thinking about mathematical problems to help his own students. He sought to make explicit ways of thinking about problems in order to use them as generalized approaches to help with the entire process of mathematical problem-solving.

How to Solve It is a resource that has come to underpin problem-solving approaches in many math curricula around the world and is embedded in the National Council of Teachers of Mathematics process documents. Much of what teachers know about teaching with and about problem-solving we learned from Polya. Generalized versions of Polya's work in teacher resources usually exist in the form of lists like this one:

1. Understand the problem. List keywords. Find mathematical language.

2. Make a plan to solve the problem.
3. Carry out the plan. Did the plan work? Do you need to change your plan?
4. Reflect on the solution. Is it correct? Is there any more work to be done?

Polya's work is an invisible force embedded in the methods of several generations of mathematics teachers. Taken for granted as it is, it is worth considering what Polya was really trying to achieve with his book.

THE STRENGTHS AND WEAKNESSES OF PROBLEM-SOLVING MODELS

Polya wrote about how to approach mathematics problems generally, but many have taken his problem-solving heuristic as a strict model for solving problems, which is then turned into a graphic organizer for students to dutifully fill in. A quick Google search would reveal many variations on the "four-step problem-solving model." If you have been in an elementary school for any length of time, then you have probably heard references to the four steps we need to take when we solve problems.

POLYA'S FOUR STEP PROBLEM-SOLVING HEURISTIC TURNED INTO A GRAPHIC ORGANIZER

Understand the problem.	Make a plan.
Carry out the plan.	Look back at the solution.

Problem-solving is a lot more complex as classroom work than just filling in a graphic organizer on command. A graphic organizer is useful for organizing our thinking and as scaffolding for our thinking, but an entire way of thinking cannot be reduced to just a method. This model is probably too prescriptive and reductive of mathematics. Thinking about problems is a way of thinking that is seamlessly embedded in the life of problem-solving classrooms. It is the life of the classroom, not something that can always be captured in a graphic organizer.

We have all seen students laboriously filling out "things we know" and taking an inordinate length of time in writing out a plan, when the reality of problem-solving is that plans can change. Problem-solving requires more adaptive rather than rigid thinking. At the end of the process, in the last box, students write out their solutions, when the work—the actual representations of the mathematics in the problem—are probably more faithful and true to the problem. The following is a simple example of a word problem that might be given to young learners and how they might use the four-step problem-solving model:

> Aidan has 6 more baseball cards than Muhammad. Together, they have 58 total baseball cards. How many baseball cards does each have?

Our students would dutifully list things they know, so in the first box, they might list "58" and "6 more," and if they have been taught to pick out keywords, then they might also list "total" and "how many" as signals that addition should be involved somehow. You can make this list without thinking very much about the problem at all. It is helpful to figure out what is known before starting, but it is can happen at the same time as solving the problem.

Students do not need to fill in boxes on an organizer to show us that they can solve problems. They need to think and to show us what they are thinking and why. Problem-solving turned into a checklist does not serve us in teaching through problem-solving classrooms. We want to think slowly, and we want to think deeply about mathematical problems. But in schools held back by schedules and time constraints, problems must be done before the bell rings, at which point they are forgotten as students get up and move to their next class.

This four-step model is reasonable as a general method, in the sense that all heuristics are general, practical, and designed to give us the greatest chance of success. Note, though, that "understand the problem" is often the most massive and lengthy part of working on any problem. For major mathematics problems, this is the longest part by far. In the world of professional mathematics, mathematicians may spend years of their life considering a line of attack or way in to a problem. "Understand the problem" is a process fraught with tension; frustration; and, indeed, frequently a lack of understanding. Whether we are comfortable in this state of not knowing is what matters.

Unfortunately for time-bound school mathematics, problems can and should be thought about slowly. Schools are in a rush to get through the required content because the curriculum says they must. But your students may have their "eureka" or "find the door" moment much later if they know they are allowed to spend more time on problems. Students often come back the next morning fresh with new insights and results on classroom tasks. "Go for a walk" and even "sleep on it" should be seen as problem-solving strategies in their own right. We need time and mental space to think about mathematics. Encourage your students to set aside a problem overnight, and they can come back to it the next day. Tell them that sometimes the best way to think about a problem is not to think about it. Advise them to revisit the problem the next day and see how much their thinking has evolved, changed, or deepened.

Polya's method should be reframed as a way of thinking mathematically about problems. We should encourage our students to develop their own ways of thinking about problems. We can help them to think heuristically by guiding them to understand their own ways of thinking about mathematics. We need to make mathematical thought processes explicit in our classrooms. We need to call attention to not just solutions, not just answers, but also the steps we take along the way. The process of analyzing a problem should be seen as just as interesting, if not more so, than getting an answer.

UNDERSTANDING HEURISTIC THINKING

Students probably have internalized their own shortcuts or ways of thinking about familiar things. Some of these familiar methods are so compressed and so routine from years of use that they are basically algorithms for living, like the process of brushing teeth or putting on clothes.

To understand heuristic thinking, consider for a moment the familiar hobby of doing jigsaw puzzles. Initially considering a jigsaw puzzle, with its hundreds or thousands of disconnected pieces sitting in a box, is difficult. It's hard to know where to begin. Veteran puzzle doers might experience what Csikszentmihalyi called "flow." After we get a feel for the puzzle, time seems to disappear, as our eyes and mind lock in to shapes, color tones, and contrasts between shapes and structures, and the puzzle begins to take shape before our mind's eye. In this state of mind, puzzle pieces almost seem to put themselves together. The most pleasurable thing that happens while you are "jigsaw puzzling" is when you pick up a piece and just see where it goes. You place it without hesitation. That often happens in the state of jigsaw puzzling deep flow. Time seems to disappear as you are in the pleasurable state of solving the problem of putting the pieces (back) together.

You learn to do jigsaw puzzles by doing jigsaw puzzles. By doing enough puzzles, you develop mental strategies and hone those strategies over time. Having done enough puzzles to be good at doing puzzles and strategizing about puzzles, we might come up with a heuristic for doing them, such as this one:

- Gather all edge pieces.
- Gather any pieces that are accidentally stuck together (there are always pairs accidentally stuck together from the factory, and they are a free gift to you, the puzzler).

- Gather all pieces of the brightest color, and start to make progress with that color.
- Gather all pieces that really stick out or are obvious because they are unique compared to the rest of the puzzle.

Our heuristic is close to being a step-by-step algorithm for doing puzzles. But we developed our algorithm by thinking while doing puzzles, not by *avoiding* thinking. Algorithms are often deployed in mathematics classrooms as "thinking proof structures" or as the automatization of thought, and there is a place for that in our mathematical training but hopefully not toward the beginning.

Consider a second familiar example: word searches. This might be the beginning of a heuristic for word searches:

- Scan the letters from left to right, starting at the first row.
- Look for double-letter combos.
- Look for less common letters, like X or Z.
- Scan for any easy-to-find words that just kind of pop out at a glance.

Sudoku is a third common example and one that is more inherently logical and mathematical in nature. Sudoku doers have practical strategies they use to give them success at doing sudoku. These might include placing digits that are still in play in the top right corner of each box and crossing them off when they are eliminated.

Thinking about how to do jigsaw puzzles or word searches or sudoku is not too hard; all three are relatively narrow and well defined, with their own rules for completion and success. We can define each as done when they are finished. But there is value in verbalizing *how* we think about jigsaw puzzles, word searches, and sudoku, and there is certainly value in verbalizing how we think about mathematics.

THE LIMITS OF HEURISTICS

Mathematics is a much bigger and more complex thing to think about than jigsaw puzzles, word searches, or sudoku. It is a massive domain of human knowledge and thought with its own facts, rules, and logical structures. In doing a problem, we need to ask ourselves questions like:

- What kind of mathematics is this?
- What tools will I use to attack this problem?
- What other problem is this problem like?

With mathematics as the object of thought, we must find ways to think about the mathematics at hand and represent that mathematics. We must bring a "new thing" into being, where that thing did not exist before.

Problem-solving is a tricky business, and heuristics can only take us so far. Unlike doing word searches or jigsaw puzzles, solving mathematics problems relies on content-specific knowledge. We must know many things about mathematics to do mathematics. In our kindergarten to grade 12 mathematics education, we learn thousands of little bits of knowledge that we must connect together and somehow use. There are no problems devoid of mathematical content; rather, problems are, as discussed already, vehicles for mathematical content.

Thinking about how novices develop their heuristics could be useful for teachers. If you do a whole bunch of jigsaw puzzles, then you will have internalized strategies for successfully doing jigsaw puzzles. You will improve at doing them. Doing lots of word searches or sudoku will make you better at completing word searches and sudoku. The more problems that our students solve, the better they will get at solving problems. The more mathematics we do, the better we will be at doing mathematics. This may seem self-evident, but we need to build our principles from the bottom up, taking nothing for granted. Do lots of mathematics to get better at mathematics. Think mathematically to get better at thinking mathematically.

A HEURISTIC FOR MOVING FROM NOVICE TO LESS NOVICE IN MATHEMATICS CLASSROOMS

So how do students make the move from being novice problem-solvers to less novice problem-solvers in mathematics classrooms? Here is a general list:

1. Do lots of mathematics problems.
2. Pay attention to the things that you do that makes solving those problems easier.
3. Use those things to help you solve problems.

This list is deliberately sparse. Teachers are there the whole time, guiding students to make sense of the mathematics at work in any problem. In this way, we are helping our students to develop their own mental model for problem-solving. Paying attention to their own thinking while doing problems is like developing their own personal heuristics for problem-solving.

To bring this list of principles to life, you obviously need to do lots of different types of problems, starting from the first day of the year or semester. Make lots of opportunities to talk about how you solve problems. Make mathematical thinking something that is seen and heard in the classroom.

Make lists of generally useful strategies, like making a table or chart. Co-create lists of those strategies and tools. Push your students to explain what they are thinking about while they solve problems. Make the process tangible and visible. Make problem-solving something that is talked about. Most of all, take every opportunity to get students to explain how they are thinking about problems. Make students aware of their own unique problem-solving processes. Make careful note of similarities in how students solve problems, but also celebrate differences—unique and personal ways of approaching and solving problems.

Items number 1 to 3 on this list are useful for any and all problem-solvers, whether they are students or not. Teachers, who are responsible for explicit teaching and modeling of the problem-solving process, can add this principle for their classrooms:

4. Talk about how you solved problems.

Mathematical knowledge itself is used in service of doing problems. We need to learn and know lots of mathematics content and develop many skills along the way as we evolve from novice to experienced mathematics students. If these little knowledge bits are fabric, then teachers are helping their students to weave them together into a tapestry, a more coherent and collected body of knowledge.

Students need robust tool kits full of things they know about mathematics in order to solve problems. In kindergarten, students start to develop their first tools, such as counting. In the primary years, they add the operations of adding, subtracting, multiplying, and dividing to their mental tool kits. As they go on in the grades, they add more sophisticated tools, like the order of operations.

BEYOND HEURISTICS

Can problem-solving skills be explicitly taught or even taught at all in any meaningful sense of the word? Depending on whom you talk to, the answer is "definitely yes" or "not at all."

Problem-solving can be explicitly taught by teaching students to pay attention to how they think about the problems in front of them. Students get better at solving problems in math class by seeing lots of different problems, experiencing the process of solving them, and having a chance to develop their own internalized problem-solving heuristics. They learn how to solve problems by listening to how others solved the same problem. They learn in a community of problem-solvers, guided by a teacher who has a firm grasp of the big ideas of mathematics at play, the curriculum, and possible ways of doing problems.

We need to get specific about ways to approach mathematical problems. There are strategies that we can explicitly show our students. Perhaps the most powerful is a strategy used at all levels of mathematics: Solve an adjacent or simpler problem. This fits our definition of *mathematical thinking*—we strip problems down into their essential elements until they are bare. Solving a simpler problem is a powerful weapon in our problem-solving arsenal. But what happens when kids can't think of a simpler or related problem to start with? Sometimes they don't know enough to make connections.

Classrooms often have generic lists of problem-solving strategies on display to help students work on problems. A problem-solving strategies list often looks something like this:

- Make a model with manipulatives.
- Draw a picture.
- Find a pattern.
- Guess and check.
- Make a table or chart.
- Make the problem simpler.
- Work backward.

All of these strategies are useful, though generic. None of them guarantees to "bring into being" a student's mathematical thinking. None of them is specific to any mathematical content, but all are useful hints about how to begin. One of these strategies might be the thing that opens the door to solving a problem just a crack. Call attention to these strategies when they are used.

In problem-solving classrooms, we talk daily about how we solved problems and how our solution paths are alike and different. We show each other our work. We compare how our work is alike and how it is different. We explain how we used our own strategies and learn from the strategies of others. We follow different solution paths to get to the same result.

Teachers must talk to students about their thinking on a regular basis, or students will not get better at problem-solving. Given lots of opportunities to think about and work on a variety of problems, our students will get better at monitoring their own thinking about mathematics.

Teachers create the conditions for "thinking about thinking" when it comes to mathematics. A metacognitive classroom is one where students are comfortable talking about how they solved problems. Teachers create metacognitive classroom cultures where students are constantly reflecting on, revising, and engaging in an inner dialogue about problems they are solving:

- Does this make sense?
- What could I do differently?

- Is there another way to approach this problem?
- How can I represent this problem on paper?
- Could I explain my thinking to a peer or to my teacher?

Problem-solving is not a linear beginning-to-end process, and it certainly is much broader and bigger than something that can fit into a graphic organizer in four steps. Problem-solving is a constant iteration of ideas, of improving on our ideas and monitoring our progress toward the solution. Polya proposes an inner dialogue with ourselves that involves repeatedly and constantly asking ourselves the following questions:

- Where should I start?
- What can I do?
- What can I gain by doing so?

Experienced problem-solvers have an inner dialogue. Experienced problem-solvers are aware of their own thinking as they solve problems and continually monitor and pay attention to their own thinking. Experienced problem-solvers constantly revise, change, and improve their problem-solving process. Teachers, as more experienced problem-solvers, guide and help their students to become aware of their own reflective thinking process as they solve problems.

REPRESENTING AND "BRINGING INTO BEING"

Axiom: Representation in mathematics classrooms is both a mental and a physical activity—one of thinking about and "bringing into being."

Moving beyond generic problem-solving strategies, we must teach our students to bring their mathematical thinking into being. Just saying "Draw me a picture" is not enough. Students in mathematics classrooms are often encouraged to show their thinking in numbers, pictures, and words. *Picture* is a bit of a misnomer here, as we really do not mean works of art but rather "representations with *mathematical content*." In mathematics classrooms, we use the discipline-based tool called mathematical thinking. Pictures with no inherent mathematics do not fit into this definition. We can better honor students' thinking by helping them, advising them, and coaching them in which tools or representations would be useful to solve a given problem.

In problem-solving classrooms, we show students how to represent mathematics on the page through words, abstract symbols and numbers, and good diagrams with mathematical content. Mathematics is also meant to be spoken of; teachers help their students to verbalize their thinking about problems. Explicit and careful instruction about which representations are useful at which time is necessary. Mental and physical models and manipulatives need to be deployed for good reasons and at the right time. When learning how to represent fractions, for example, students can be shown how to represent fractions as parts of a set (for example, 4 out of the 10 objects are cubes, and 6 are spheres), with linear models (like a ruler or along a piece of string), using two dimensions (like arrays and open-area rectangles), and with three-dimensional models (like filling containers). Representing fractions with familiar objects like cookies or pie and with concrete counting objects comes first. As students develop their understanding of one-, two-, and three-dimensional space, they can start to use those models. In our understanding of mathematics, we generally move from concrete to abstract, and teachers help to gauge the appropriate level of abstraction needed when representing a problem. Being purposeful in teaching about representations helps students to know how and when they are useful. Teachers show students how representations *work*.

Why is a rectangle a good way to show a fraction like 2/5? (It is easy to accurately divide the total space, which is one whole. Circles are tricky because the arc on the end of each slice makes it hard to divide and judge which fraction we are looking at.) Is a container half full of water the same as a piece of string marked halfway along? (Yes, because a full container is one whole, and the length of the string is also one whole.)

THE PROCESS OF REPRESENTING MATHEMATICS

Students must be taught ways of representing mathematics. They must learn to bring their thinking about mathematical problems into the world. *Representing mathematics is defined as thinking about a mathematical object, problem, or task and bringing it into being in the world, either on paper, in words, or by manipulating physical objects.* Mental representations can become physical representations. Thinking is brought out into the open in problem-solving classrooms, which are open spaces for thought, unbounded, like the mind of Hamlet even as he felt "bounded in a nutshell." In reality, he had infinite space, and so do our students, if we don't constrain them too much.

Consider Pape and Tchoschanov's (2001) definition of *representation*: "We use the term representation(s) to refer to both the internal and external manifestations of mathematical concepts. We write representation(s) with the parenthetical 's' to emphasize that . . . we are speaking of both the act of representing (the verb, to represent) and the external form of the representation (the noun form)." *Representation* is both a verb and a noun.

Consider the example of the number 6. A child learns to count to six, as they develop an internal mental image of six and then connect it to sets of six countable objects and then to the written numeral *6*. This child begins to develop their sense of "sixness" and to be able to bring "sixness" into the world by counting six objects, knowing there are a total of six objects (cardinality of a set) and knowing that *6* represents "sixness." A considerable process of development, growth, and change in mental and physical representation occurs as children learn to count.

Consider also the familiar curricular goal of "learning times tables." Students can become familiar with their multiplication facts by rote. This condition may be characterized by flash cards, repetition, and verbalizing the product. In this learning condition, a teacher says, "9 × 8," and students nearly instantly reply, "72." Indeed, many learn multiplication through flashcards, so they have an underdeveloped set of mental imagery for times tables. Some people just "see" arrays of 9 × 8 objects or have other interesting imagery attached to single-digit multiplication. Others have strategies to derive facts when, for some reason, those facts don't stick in their long-term memories. In this case they might have a near fact memorized, like 9 × 7 or 9 × 9, and add or subtract one group to get an answer. If you have worked with this number fact enough, then it will be stored in your long-term memory. Most students are able to commit number facts to long-term memory after using them enough. Some students, if asked, will tell you that 9 × 8 is a "known fact." But how do they know it, and what do they know about it?

ATTACHING IMAGERY TO MULTIPLICATION

It is useful in teaching multiplication to help students to attach some imagery to a fact to make it more representational (see figure 3.1). Or, you could ask them to consider 9 rows of 8 objects or 8 rows of 9 objects, neatly arrayed, and to construct this array from counting objects if it helps them.

Two Models For Multiplying

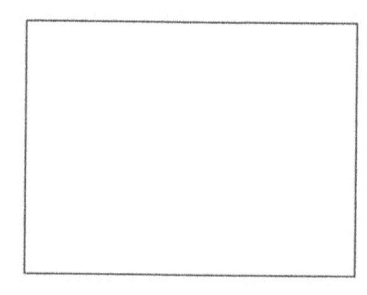

If this is a 9 x 8 rectangle, can you imagine it rotated 90° on to its side? Is it still the same rectangle?

If this arrow is 9 units long, can you imagine this arrow stretching 8 times, like an elastic band?

Figure 3.1. There are many ways to think about multiplication.

We have under consideration the dual nature of mathematical representation, as both the act of representing and the representation itself. Again, representation is both a verb and a noun. This quite neatly corresponds to the current National Council of Teachers of Mathematics (NCTM) definition of *representation*: as both a process and as a product.

REPRESENTATION IN THE NCTM PROCESS STANDARDS

Instructional programs from prekindergarten through grade 12 should enable each and every student to—

- Create and use representations to organize, record, and communicate mathematical ideas.
- Select, apply, and translate among mathematical representations to solve problems.
- Use representations to model and interpret physical, social, and mathematical phenomena.

Create is the key word in this process standard. Creation is "bringing into being," which is how we approach representation in problem-solving classrooms. Teachers guide this process of creation, helping students to build mental models and imagery, and advising them on which representations would be useful, at which times, and on which problems. Teachers ensure that students are exposed to multiple representations of mathematical concepts and that they understand how these representations work.

The process of thinking about how to represent a problem leads to the product, a representation of that problem. *Thinking* is the verb, or action of doing a problem; a *mathematical representation* is the noun, or product of that action. We need to help our students to visualize representations of interesting mathematical concepts in order to imagine them into being.

As students advance in mathematics, we should encourage representational thinking; that is, building and having a repertoire of ways to externalize math concepts. Tables, graphs, tree diagrams, area models, arrays are all examples of representations they can learn to use.

The end goal of representation, at least from a teacher assessment perspective, is good communication. Can the students communicate their thinking in words or on paper using mathematical representations? How do different representations show the same math in different ways?

Fluency with multiple representations should be a goal of problem-solving classrooms; we can help students to visualize, conceptualize, and make real their understanding of powerful mathematics. Mathematical thinkers have adopted the identity of mathematical thinkers. They learn how to approach problems, to represent them, and to bring them from their minds into the world. Representation is both the act of thinking about mathematics and the creation of those representations in our world.

Chapter Four

The Mutually Complementary Nature of Procedural and Conceptual Understanding

Axiom: Basic skills and problem-solving (procedural and conceptual understanding) are not at odds but rather are mutually complementary.

Consider as the object of your thought this expression: 1,003 − 998. Depending on how you were schooled, you are not used to taking an expression like "1,003 − 998" as an object of thought. Addition expressions are things to be dealt with quickly, to be gotten out of the way. Your training in school would probably lead you to stack the numbers on top of each other and carry out the standard algorithm. If we know how to use the standard algorithm for addition, then this would probably take us between five and ten seconds. The standard algorithm is compact, efficient, time tested, and a virtual guarantee of correctness if all its steps are carried out in the correct way, in the correct order.

But why would you need to carry out the standard algorithm here? The number 998 is only 5 away from 1,003. It might be better to reverse the expression and add 2 to make 1,000 and then add 3, for a total of 5 added. It might be better to imagine traveling forward or backward on a number line 5 units, from 998 or from 1,003.

Consider another example with multiplication: 12 × 22. Knowing how to use the standard multiplication algorithm well, you would carry out a procedure with steps you can verbalize like this:

- "2 times 2 is 4."
- "2 times 1 is 2."

- "Put a 0 in the bottom right of the second row or an empty space, depending on how you were trained)."
- "2 times 2 is 4."
- "2 times 1 is 2."
- "4 plus 0 is 4. 4 plus 2 is 6. 2 plus 0 is 2."
- "The answer is 264."

It is useful to have all our knowledge of multiplication consolidated into one working algorithm that spits out the correct answer every single time. The standard algorithm for multiplication is generally stored in our long-term memories, to be accessed when needed. We see two-digit-by-two-digit multiplication and retrieve from long-term memory the steps we must follow, nearly without thinking. This automaticity becomes a powerful advantage as we progress in our mathematics education. Automaticity aids working memory and allows us to deal with more advanced calculations with more steps. Algorithms are powerful tools that we can and should use in mathematics, but they should not be given to students without proper preparation and conceptual teaching.

There is no rush to get to using standard algorithms. There is time and space in the early years to build a conceptual foundation for all the operations before we learn to use procedures. Kindergarten and grades 1 and 2 are the time to build this foundation, starting from counting. We learn to count by rote at first and then proceed to use the fact $1 + 1$ as the basis for adding, which leads us in turn to its opposite, subtracting. More advanced knowledge of skip-counting and grouping leads us to multiplication, which in turn has its own inverse, division. All four basic operations are interesting in their own right as objects of thought. Automation of procedures in the form of algorithmic knowledge can come later, after we have built our conceptual foundation.

BUILDING A CONCEPTUAL UNDERSTANDING OF MULTIPLICATION

Consider building this conceptual basis for multiplication. In your classroom, you will have carefully scaffolded and built your students a broad understanding of multiplication, using tools like arrays and the area model as a good conceptual base on which the algorithm can sit on. You will have considered the case for multiplication as repeated addition. The students will have considered problems that require grouping and practiced skip-counting by various multiples. They will have torn apart the first few highly composite numbers, 12 and 24, to see how they work. To proceed from a strict definition, your students will know that 12 times 22 means "12 copies of 22," if you proceed from the precise definition of "multiplier times multiplicand." What does it mean to have 12 copies of 22 objects?

In the last chapter, I used 51 × 25 as an object of thought. Hopefully you felt successful as you thought about it. Now let's try again, taking 12 times 22 as the object of thought. Pause and consider this multiplication expression. Take all that you know about multiplication, and take all that you know about the numbers we call *12* and *22*, and bring your mathematical thought to bear on this expression. What imagery do you have in your mind? Can you think of a way to carry out this calculation in your mind? Do you have any grouping strategies that helped you get the answer? Did you scribble anything down on paper?

It is not beyond your calculating powers to do two-digit-by-two-digit multiplication in your head, trust me. Training our minds to carry out mental operations is empowering, and it is pleasurable. Calculations are often thought of as something just to "get through," and at times we may have a need for speed, but calculations can be pleasurable in their own right. Visualize, now, an empty rectangle, 22 units by 12 units (see figure 4.1). Rotate it as you need to in your mind to get it oriented just right. How many different ways could you divide this rectangle to get the answer to this multiplying expression?

You might also consider that you are going to give your students an "algorithm license," permission to use the algorithm ever after if they can show how and why it works. This is a bit different from acquiring a driver's license: You do not need to know how the car works to drive it. You do not

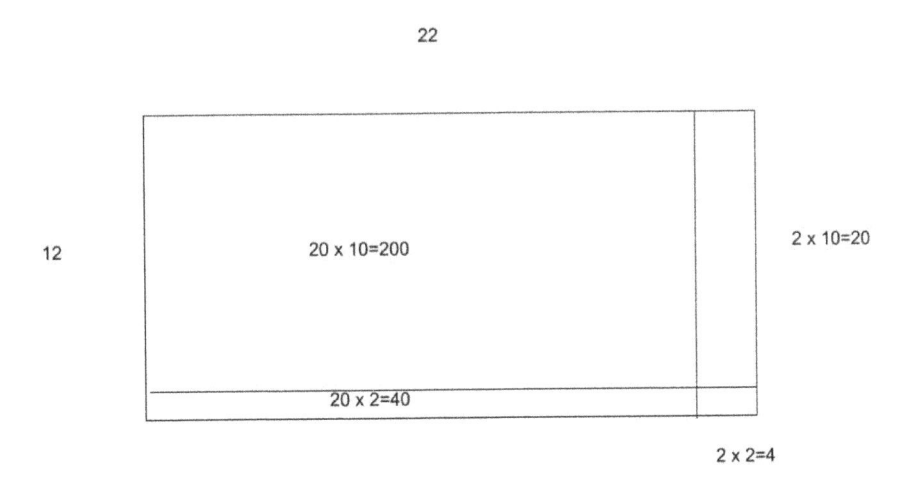

Figure 4.1. The standard algorithm visualized as a subdivided rectangle to show partial products.

need to know how the standard algorithm for multiplication works to use it, but it is more *interesting* to know. An algorithm license is granted to our students after they have built a strong conceptual foundation for the operation under consideration. Show me that you know how the operation works, show me that you know what it *is*, and then you may use the standard algorithm.

The multiplication algorithm works by totaling partial products. Were you shown that in school? Let's hope so—and let's show our students how the standard algorithm works. The algorithm is a marvel of compression—it compresses all the partial products into one nifty procedure that uses addition of partial products to get the final result. Taking the time to decompress the algorithm and show why it works will give our students the best of both worlds: a powerful sense of procedural fluency combined with an understanding of the concept at work.

You probably did not think of it this way, but imagine an elastic band, 22 units long. This might be a rather long elastic band, depending on which unit you are imagining. Perhaps it is 22 inches, less than two feet long. Imagine it stretching out to 12 times its original length. How long is the elastic band now? Can you imagine now that you are standing beside it, taking steps of exactly 22 inches 12 times until you get to the end? A stretching elastic band is an interesting mental visual model for multiplication.

The visual representations (the elastic band and the rectangle) are identical in mathematical content to the abstract representation (the symbols for the numbers used in the standard algorithm). They are different models for the same thing. Applying an algorithm with the powerful understanding of how it works is the best-case scenario for our students. Spend the necessary time on building an understanding of how an algorithm works, and then unleash your students with this empowering understanding. An algorithm license is valid for life, but you cannot get one without building a strong and wide conceptual base for operations.

"KNOWING" AND "UNDERSTANDING" MATHEMATICS

Knowledge, skill, and *understanding* are three commonly used but debatable and even misunderstood terms in education. They are so overused and sometimes misused to be almost devoid of meaning, but they are necessary for the work of teaching. Teachers often throw these words around without consideration for how they might be the same or different.

Knowledge is simply retrieving information or facts from our long-term memory. Skills in mathematics classrooms are routine performances, often defined in terms of skills with calculations (carrying out calculations) or skills with making graphs (making scales, labeling axes) or skills with manipulating algebraic expressions (solving for x), to give just a few examples.

Understanding is one of the trickiest terms to deal with in the education world because it attempts to describe a mental process. Understanding could be said to be the mental process of one who comprehends something. *Understanding* is often differentiated in the education world from *knowledge*. *Knowledge* may come first, but *understanding* is better, so our thinking goes. We can gather an inert set of facts, like the names of US presidents, without knowing anything about them. We can know their dates of birth and even the names of important legislation they passed while still knowing little about the time in which they lived or the political context in which they worked. To assemble through our mental processes a coherent body of knowledge about a topic is to gain understanding. All of us have coherent bodies of knowledge about certain things, perhaps about US presidents or Pokémon or snakes. We have gained an understanding about these things by gathering knowledge and fitting that knowledge together into something resembling a coherent whole.

We come to understand mathematics by pulling together all the things we know about mathematics into something that is the most coherent and concrete mental whole we can make. In their kindergarten to grade 12 education, our students constantly organize and reorganize their knowledge about mathematics. They build and rebuild their schema for mathematics to accommodate new knowledge "bits." They weave together these discrete things, and we help them.

One example is the process of learning about number itself. Young children learn to count with whole numbers. Then they learn there is another type of number called fractions, which they might or might not be told are rational numbers. Their schema for number later expands to include real numbers (decimals) and then further branches into rational and irrational numbers (like pi, for example). They can perform operations on all these numbers, although it might initially seem tricky to do so. They also learn about integers, which means they can now count below zero and perform operations on negative numbers as well. Clearly, we need a flexible and broad base for our understanding of *number* itself, a word whose meaning is never fixed, changing over the course of our students' K–12 education as they learn about different types of numbers.

The US Common Core Standards offers this definition of *mathematical understanding*:

> But what does mathematical understanding look like? One hallmark of mathematical understanding is the ability to justify, in a way appropriate to the student's mathematical maturity, why a particular mathematical statement is true or where a mathematical rule comes from. There is a world of difference between a student who can summon a mnemonic device to expand a product

such as (a + b) (x + y) and a student who can explain where the mnemonic comes from. (Common Core State Standards Initiative 2015)

We owe it to our students to help with this process of sense making. We owe it to our students to show them *why* certain rules and procedures are true. We owe it to our students to present mathematics as more than just lists of things to be memorized. Memorization is often a condition of learning. If we work enough with mathematics facts, then we will remember those mathematics facts, but it is not usually a specific goal of learning. Memory can be considered what is created by thinking. If we think about certain things enough, then we will remember them.

There is a point at which certain things become stored in our long-term memories. The process of changing our cognitive architecture to fit in new things is the process of learning itself. There is seemingly no limit to the number of things we can fit in (and many humans are capable of astounding feats of memorization, like the many thousands of digits of pi), but discrete and disconnected knowledge bits will fall out of our minds. They will disappear like smoke if not used. How many of the formulae or equations you memorized in school do you remember? A few? None? Likely not all of them. If you don't use it, then you forget it.

There is a seemingly never-ending debate about how best to learn times tables. Maybe we should substitute *knowing* for *memorizing*. If we work enough with our times tables and build a robust understanding of multiplication in general, then those times tables facts will probably stick in our long-term memories.

Memorization is not a goal of mathematics classrooms in and of itself, but rather it can be a by-product of the process of learning. Simply put, if we do enough mathematics, then we will remember the mathematics we do. We might not set out to memorize our times tables or use flash cards to drill them into our brains, but the more we use them, in games or in context of interesting problems, the more we will remember them. How many times do you need to see "7×7" before it sticks in your long-term memory? Probably not as many as you think. Further, patterns help; if you know your 2s, then you know your 4s, and if you know your 3s, then you know your 6s. Not having your times tables memorized is not something to be ashamed of. Some of us simply cannot commit them to long-term memory. What matters is having strategies for getting unstuck when we blank on a number fact.

The 7s and 9s are often the hardest to know. Many of us get stuck on facts like 8×7 or 9×7 and fall back on strategies to derive the answer, and that is fine. We need to come to know numbers on a more-than-rote basis. We should be on a friendly basis with numbers, not afraid of them. Timed tests and "Mad Minute" exercises, mad scrambles to write down as many facts as you can in a short length of time, only build fear and loathing in students who are not fast.

Our goal is knowing, and instant retrieval of facts is no guarantee of knowing. You can come to know a number like 64 as 8 × 8 or as a whole bunch of 2s, or you can come to know 64 as one group of 8 less than 72. As you come to know 64, you come to understand what makes it unique.

The late Grant Wiggins (2014) offers this definition of *understanding*: "In a phrase, understanding is the ability to think and act flexibly with what one knows. To put it another way, an understanding of a topic is a 'flexible performance capability,' with emphasis on the flexible. Performing mathematics in a flexible way is a goal of problem-solving classrooms." Thinking flexibly about mathematics while doing and representing mathematics is the best-case scenario for our students; carrying out procedures with seemingly random knowledge bits that do not fit into a broader schema or understanding is the worst-case scenario. Random, disconnected things will be soon forgotten. Things we have stored in our long-term memories but don't use will be forgotten. Chances are, you have forgotten the phone number of your best friend from elementary school if it was long enough ago.

In mathematics, knowing without understanding is often characterized as a state in which our students have memorized sets of facts and procedures to be dutifully used on tests and assessments and possibly forgotten soon after they are performed or used. Sets of facts are not as useful if they are not connected to a bigger and wider understanding about the topic at hand. Disconnected facts are often forgotten. If you do not use the periodic table of elements in your daily work, you have perhaps forgotten most things about the periodic table of elements. *Au* stands for gold, it is true, but what characterizes gold?

In the multiplication example, knowing how to apply the standard algorithm for multiplication is no guarantee that we know how it works. Knowing what multiplication is and having access to visual representations for and possible definitions of multiplication is a better scenario. Multiplication connects to a wider web of knowledge and becomes something that is understood as much as just known. The broader mental landscape in which multiplication exists is connected all the way back to counting and all the way forward to exponentiation, factorials, quadratic expressions, and so on. This broad landscape includes all our models, or ways of seeing and knowing, multiplication.

It is debatable whether we can or should break *knowledge* and *understanding* into two separate constructs. When students attain understanding, how is this different than acquiring knowledge? Is it any different? Depth is often given as a marker for how well we understand a given topic. This metaphor works to some extent: Loose, disconnected facts just lie on the surface, like leaves in fall, waiting to be gathered together. What lies beneath? Is there a beneath? Facts, when gathered together, allow us to go deeper. A deeper understanding is what we want in our problem-solving classrooms.

Depth, however, is perhaps an illusion. We are not really talking about a deep dive into ocean depths or tunneling beneath the surface. We are really talking about connecting loose and scattered and disconnected knowledge bits together into something resembling a coherent whole. This is a gestalt: an organized whole that is more than the sum of its parts. It is a state of understanding.

I live in a state of strong understanding of the collected works of the singer, poet, and song-and-dance man Bob Dylan. This understanding is very complex, detailed, and organized. It includes both minutiae, trivia about him, and an awareness of bigger and wider themes in his artistic works. I am familiar with his recorded works, his biography, his writing process, his skill on various instruments, and his live recordings. You probably have something you have your own gestalt about, whether its mathematics or baking cookies or the history of the NCAA basketball tournament. To reach such a state of understanding is empowering, but it takes time. A gestalt of mathematics should be the goal of mathematics curricula across the world.

PROCEDURAL AND CONCEPTUAL UNDERSTANDING IN MATHEMATICS CLASSROOMS

Procedural understanding and *conceptual understanding* are typically set off from each other as polar opposites in debates over how best to teach mathematics. We have a perceived dichotomy in the mathematics education community between the two, which are often seen as competing, with priority in traditional classrooms often given to procedural understanding. In turn, more conceptual pedagogical approaches are often deemed fuzzy, sloppy, imprecise, and too constructivist to build a sound knowledge base in our students.

A procedure is a sequence of steps that can be taken, often in service of answer getting. Procedural knowledge is frequently derided as surface or "lesser" knowledge, and in some cases and in some ways, it is. *Procedural understanding* can be simply defined as knowing how to apply rules and procedures in mathematics, with or without knowing why they work. A related construct is procedural fluency or skill, with fluency being the ability to carry out procedures. If you know the procedures, then you can carry them out accurately.

Mathematics education is infamously full of procedures like the multiplication and division of fractions that are often simply given as rules to be followed: "Ours is not to reason why; just invert and multiply." Giving an oversimplified rule like this one is depriving students of a chance to really

Procedural and Conceptual Understanding 55

know and understand what is happening when they divide two fractions. The idea that multiplication makes numbers bigger falls apart, and our students with a fragile conceptual base for multiplication will find that they hit a wall here.

Fraction multiplication, for example "1/3 × 1/4," can be taught as simply "multiply the numerators, then multiply the denominators." But why does this work? Likewise, we might find for ourselves that "1/2 ÷ 1/4" is too conceptually tricky to teach, and our own understanding of the meaning of the operation is too fragile or nonexistent, so we fall back on tricks: "Ours is not to reason why; just invert and multiply!" Rules expire, and they break, and we need a flexible base of conceptual understanding that can fit new and expanding definitions and rules, such as the idea that multiplying two fractions makes a smaller fraction.

A visual representation would help us to make sense of fraction multiplication and division. Can you picture, in the first case, that a 1/3 multiplier is actually making 1/4 shrink? Picture an elastic band of 1/4 length. It has shrunk back to 1/3 of its original length. It is now 1/12 of what it once was. In the second case, take a number line. Mark one whole at the endpoint of the line, and then mark 1/2. Can you now divide up that 1/2 segment into units of 1/4? How many do you have? Only two. The answer must be 2 (see figure 4.2).

For division, you just flipped the 4 and divided by 2. But can you explain why "invert and multiply" works? What is a reciprocal? Can you explain that to your students? Learning and showing your students how each and every rule works will help them to build a broad conceptual base. Memorized rules and tricks will be sooner forgotten. ("Ours is not to reason why; just invert and multiply" rhymes, making it more memorable and perhaps more sticky, but it is still better to show your students how it works). A procedure deployed without taking the time to build a visual and representation foundation is just another disconnected fact to be deployed without reason or understanding. This is not a learning condition we want for our students in problem-solving classrooms.

Having conceptual understanding is seeing the interconnectedness of mathematical concepts and being able to pull together discrete facts and models into something resembling a coherent whole. Having conceptual

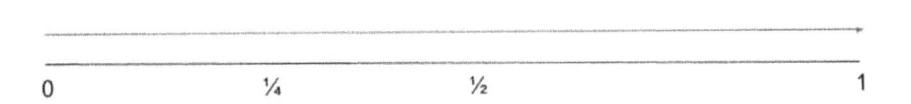

0 ¼ ½ 1

Figure 4.2. What other multiplication or division expressions are shown in this diagram?

understanding about an area of mathematics is knowing the *how* and the *why* something works.

PROCEDURAL VERSUS CONCEPTUAL UNDERSTANDING: A FALSE DICHOTOMY

Many curriculum documents and books play up the contrast between these two types of understanding, as if they are categories or containers or their own distinct worlds, with hard and fast boundaries. The media picks up this contrast, and on social media, we see examples of the so-called new math causing much debate and confusion. Each new example goes viral, and another argument about math teaching and learning begins. One famous example concerned representing 5×3 as repeated addition. A student wrote "5 + 5 + 5" and was marked wrong. The image was widely circulated on the internet. (The teacher wrote "3 + 3 + 3 + 3 + 3" beside as the correct answer, based on the formal definition of multiplying as "multiplier times multiplicand"). Formally speaking, "5 copies of 3" is more correct here, but the answer still comes out to 15, and you could prove that by drawing a 5×3 rectangle and rotating it on to its side (the commutative property of multiplication). Debates like this are very common in the social media era. Sides are taken. You might be for the Common Core or against it. You might have come to believe that students are not being taught conceptually enough, with classrooms and curricula full of routinized, nonthinking, procedural tasks and worksheets. You might think that traditional mathematics education is producing legions of mathematical robots, unthinking automatons who know only facts and procedures. These are the children schooled in old ways, unsuited for the world of twenty-first century skills, not trained to think and stumped by nonroutine problems, so the thinking goes.

Or, conversely, you might believe that traditional mathematics education is being disrupted in favor of well-meaning but "fuzzy" approaches that prioritize multiple solution paths, explaining solutions in words, and leaving students without a grasp of basic facts. These fuzzy math graduates are the ones who are unable to make change for a ten-dollar bill and stumble over simple facts like 4×6. These are the children of John Dewey—the product of more than a century of "progressive" child-centered education.

Generally speaking, educators can and do believe in the priority of one approach over the other. One can self-identify broadly as "traditional" or "progressive," but in practice, few educators would adopt such confining labels. Swing too far in either direction, though, and you might feel like you are not teaching the right way, depending on the political climate of your school board or district. You might feel like you are an educational rebel on either side, depending on your organizational and pedagogical culture. You might feel shunned for "doing it wrong," so you close your door and teach because teaching is what teachers do. We teach who we are, and it is incumbent on all educators to think clearly about where they stand on how to teach mathematics. Leaving aside caricatures and stereotypes of "old" and "new" math, we have the chance to shape the very conception of the meaning of *mathematics* in our students' heads.

There are very few, if any, mathematical ideas that shouldn't be presented in a powerful visual and conceptual way. I previously discussed how to introduce the Pythagorean relationship. In a one-hour block of instructional time, you can develop a visual anchor for the formula, a visual proof, and you will then be ready to use the formula. We move from the visual and geometric to the abstract and algebraic within a class period or two, and we can then understand an algebraic relationship that is always true for all right-angled triangles, namely that the square on the hypotenuse is equal to the sum of the squares on the other two sides. Building an understanding of the concept is given priority over the development of the procedure.

But is it wrong to just write a few worked examples on your blackboard or whiteboard as you start to work with a new formula? If we proceed from several worked examples of the theorem, then are our students any better or worse off? Because you get to the same place in the end, it is probably simply a lot less interesting to start from a procedural place. In problem-solving classrooms, we develop broad conceptual bases for all topics, wherever and whenever possible.

THE ITERATIVE AND BACK-AND-FORTH RELATIONSHIP BETWEEN PROCEDURAL AND CONCEPTUAL UNDERSTANDING

Learning mathematics requires weaving together relevant facts; having a good command of processes, procedures, and skills; and possessing a conceptual understanding of the mathematics we use. Our students do not typically exist in an either/or state with regard to procedural and conceptual understanding but rather swing back and forth between the two, depending on the order of the instructional sequence deployed by the teacher. This "swinging back and forth" or iteration between the procedural and conceptual conditions of doing mathematics has been studied by Rittle-Johnson, Siegler, and Alibali (2001). Their experimental design dealt with decimal fractions on a number line but could have implications for all mathematics teaching and learning: "We propose that conceptual and procedural knowledge develop iteratively, with increases in one type of knowledge leading to increases in the other type of knowledge, which triggers new increases in the first." Improving procedural or conceptual knowledge leads students to the same place: being better able to represent a problem, which is the goal of problem-solving classrooms.

Consider our previous example of beginning a unit with young students on multiplication. Here are four possible instructional paths to get students knowing and understanding multiplication:

1. You could "just" teach the standard algorithm and then play with different conceptions of multiplication (repeated addition, the area model, and scaling, for example).
2. You could teach using arrays, then progress to using the area model, and consolidate it into the standard algorithm.
3. You could spend some time exploring mental multiplication, skip-counting, the area model, grouping, and so on, and finally, a while later, get to the standard algorithm.
4. You could deploy the standard algorithm as one strategy among many and play concurrently with different strategies, models, and meanings of multiplication.

The big promise of the back-and-forth, or iterative, model for teachers is how tight the iterations could be in any given period of instructional time. Any given mathematics period (let's say a sixty-minute chunk of time) could feature a number of back-and-forth pedagogical "moves" between procedural and conceptual understanding. Orchestrating these moves is the art of pedagogy. The purposeful and intentional orchestration of these moves is instructional design. The art of pedagogy is the minute-by-minute decision making that teachers do, responsive to the thinking of their students. It is what teachers are best at. It is what teachers are trained to do and what teachers practice every single day of their working lives.

Conceptual and procedural knowledge do not develop in an all-or-nothing way, with acquisition of one type of knowledge necessarily preceding the other. If you teach a fourth-grade class, for example, then your students might come in already knowing how to use the standard algorithm for multiplication, with little of the attached conceptual knowledge about multiplication we know is important. There is nothing stopping you from taking that student "backward" and showing them different meanings of multiplication and how the standard algorithm works. The conceptual base does, however, make later procedural work much easier.

It is fine if your students in grade 2 encounter an expression like "51 + 19" and automatically stack the numbers into the standard algorithm; you can work with that. But why not slow them down and explore "making 10" (put the 1 and 9 together and you have a 10), moving along number lines, and the idea of place value itself? The algorithm is important and useful and generally our end goal, but why not play along the way? Being in one state of knowledge about a certain mathematical topic or concept or skill does not close the door to the other. It is best not to downplay either type of knowledge or to take one side or the other but rather to acknowledge the complex bidirectional relationship between them. It is never going to be an either/or situation. One will not strictly precede the other at all times. Our pedagogical moves should reflect this complex interplay between procedural and conceptual understanding.

Procedural knowledge can precede conceptual knowledge, and conceptual knowledge can precede procedural knowledge. If you know any young children, then you know that they tend to learn the rote counting sequence before they understand the principles of counting. Counting is an example of culturally embedded rote learning—we could not avoid it if we tried, nor should we want to. Purposeful development of counting as a set of conceptual principles leading to arithmetic is the job of teachers. We would not deny our students the use of the rote counting sequence they have learned, but we will check to see that they are developing as counters and are able to use counting for specific purposes in our problem-solving classrooms.

There are times in mathematics to play with big, open concepts and ideas, and there are times to consolidate those ideas into procedures. Near the beginning, when we are starting to look at a mathematical idea or concept, is when we need to open a big, wide conceptual base for understanding. Ideas and concepts should be presented in intriguing ways that make students want to learn more. Our ultimate goal is better problem representation—having our students in the state called "understanding," where they can bring all their powerful knowledge to bear on the interesting problems and tasks we give them.

It can be difficult, if not impossible, to advance in mathematics without conceptual knowledge. It can be difficult, if not impossible, to advance in mathematics without access to basic facts and skills. An elusive and difficult-to-find balance between the two is necessary in problem-solving classrooms. In Daniel Willingham's words, "If students fail to gain conceptual understanding, it will become harder and harder to catch up, as new conceptual knowledge depends on the old. Students will become more and more likely to simply memorize algorithms and apply them without understanding" (2009–2010). A strong conceptual base is required to progress in mathematics. However, as Hattie, Fisher, and Frey (2017) point out, "when content is new, all of us have a limited understanding." They characterize "surface learning" as initial learning of concepts and skills but not in any kind of shallow way. It is neither about applying rote skills or algorithms without meaning, nor is it about trying to reach a depth of thinking too soon. It is about striking the right instructional balance at the right time as we progress toward a deeper understanding.

Chapter Five

Full Instructional Guidance and Deliberate Practice

Axiom: Full instructional guidance is a necessary condition of problem-solving classrooms.

We are more than twenty-five years into "reform" mathematics curricula, which started with the publication of the National Council of Teachers of Mathematics (NCTM) standards (1989) and has deeper roots in the "new math" after *Sputnik* was launched by Russia in 1957. Debates over how best to teach mathematics still spark emotion, urgency, and often anger. The debate is in large part over how much teacher-led direct instruction to give and when. The debate is over *how* to give direct instruction or if it is often even advisable. The argument is one that concerns the role or status of teachers themselves. Opinions on the use of direct instructional guidance are many, varied, and personal.

The oversimplified media debate is usually characterized as being between "back to basics" advocates, who want to give full explanations of topics before students are set to work, and "reform" or "discovery" mathematics advocates, who we are told often refrain from giving enough help at all. Full instructional guidance as imperative in problem-solving classrooms is discussed earlier in this book. Students, as novices, should not be left in a state of confusion for longer than is productive. Teachers, as more experienced thinkers about mathematics, decide when to give that guidance.

There are very personal choices to be made, and you could spend your own infinity grappling with how best to teach mathematics. There are many competing and complicated pedagogical theories of mathematics out there—so many that we can forgive teachers for being confused. There are no universal "best practices" guaranteed to work in all classrooms, but there are better and worse practices for given students, mathematical topics, and certain stages of mathematical development. The question, educator, is not "how best to teach"; it is how best for *you* to teach.

We teach who we are. We all have strengths, weaknesses, and things we do better or worse in our classrooms. An honest and open self-assessment of one's pedagogical strengths is necessary for reflective practitioners. I am a teacher, and after fifteen years, my own pedagogical principles for myself are simple:

- Know the curriculum, and know the important and big ideas of the mathematics behind it in order to show and explain them to students.
- Give interesting math tasks, questions, and problems, and let students play, reason, conjecture, wonder, and think.
- Embrace the mess of the problem-solving process—listen and talk to students as they do interesting mathematics.
- Be responsive to students' thinking as they develop as young thinkers about mathematics.

If pushed, each principle could be fleshed out, made more fulsome and technical, but this in plain language is a pedagogy of teaching mathematics. What's yours?

DESIGNING INSTRUCTIONAL PATHS

Designing an instructional path through a mathematical course of study is not easy work. Teachers combine the what (curriculum) with the how (pedagogy) in the day-by-day process we call lesson planning. One cannot be separated from the other. Curriculum feeds pedagogy, and pedagogy brings curriculum to life.

Lesson planning needs to be responsive and not programmatic and prescriptive while still reaching a certain end point (the reporting period or the end of semester or end of year). There are still schools out there where the entirety of a year's teaching is sitting in dusty, old binders; on dusty, old shelves; in dusty, old rooms. Visit the math prep room in an older high school, and see what you find. Many older schools still have fifty- or sixty-year-old textbooks sitting on shelves. Take one down off the shelf and flip it open. You will probably recognize the concepts from your own, more current instructional materials. Mathematics—the discipline—is modern and technical, a constantly advancing science and art. School mathematics, however, can seem frozen in time. Euler, Newton, and Gauss would recognize much of what we still do in our classrooms.

You may, in your career, have seen binders full of numbered worksheets, marked for each of days 1 through 190 in the school year. These still do exist in the form of scripted direct-instruction programs. If teaching were that easy, then we could just open to the 134th worksheet for the 134th day of school and not have to think much about what we are doing that day. "Day 134 is fraction addition. Here are twelve worked examples, kids, now you try numbers 1 to 53, odds only!" The reality of teaching and learning is that it takes many twists and turns, and while it is possible to plot a general path through a year's course of study, we still need to be responsive to the unique needs of the class in front of us. The temptation, with curriculum and assessment and reporting demands, is to take the shortest and easiest path toward the instructional goal. But, if we don't have to think much about what we are teaching, then our students probably don't have to think much about what they are learning.

AN OPEN, INQUIRY APPROACH

Mathematics teaching could be said to be the art of making trade-offs between direct instruction and exploration as we guide students toward understanding, application, and use of mathematical ideas, skills, and concepts. It is a finely orchestrated journey of knowing your students: each and every one of them. It is knowing their strengths and weaknesses and getting to know how they think about mathematics. There is considerable variation in how this is done, whether through a more traditional direct-instruction approach or a more open "inquiry" approach.

Inquiry, for our purposes, is defined simply as "asking for information." We want our students to ask for information. We want them to be so interested in the problems and tasks we give them that they are practically begging for more information to be revealed. Inquiry is a state of question-asking and curiosity. Mathematics classrooms can and should be curious classrooms, with students needing to know what the what, how, and why of big mathematical ideas. They should be active inquiry classrooms, with students attempting to pierce the very heart of the mathematical ideas under consideration.

Here is some mathematics that you and your students could inquire into. The massive size of massive numbers is something our students tend to be curious about. Many good problems begin with something about money. How much is a lot of money? How big is a million or a billion, really? Can we build an experience of these very large numbers into our sense of numbers that have been developing since birth? Bill Gates was born in 1955. His personal fortune is around $85 billion at the time of this writing. (If you are not interested in Mr. Gates, then you could also simply Google "richest person in the world" on the day you read this and use as the subject of your problem whoever is richest on that day.) How much money would he have to give away every day to give away his fortune by age seventy? Eighty? Ninety? If you dropped a hundred-dollar bill in front of Mr. Gates, would he pick it up? Is a penny worth more to you than a hundred-dollar bill is to Bill Gates? How would you approach these related problems? How would students you know handle these problems? Which formulation of the problem about billions is most interesting to you? Or do you want to ask an entirely different problem to get your students thinking about the size of billions?

What would your students do if you gave them a version of these problems? Would they be puzzled, stumped, throw up their hands? Or would they join us in the creative and beautiful mess we call problem-solving? If students know they will be challenged and they will be asked to think, then they will accept our challenges, and they will give us their best mathematical thoughts and ideas. Give them a specific formulation of this problem, so they have a place to begin, a concrete starting point. Try this one:

> If the richest person alive started to give away his fortune today at a rate of $1,000 per day, how long would it take for him or her to give all his or her money away?

Even better, we could have students generate their own set of questions and solve them. Let them truly inquire into the meaning of *billions*. Let them play with the massive, mind-bending size of these numbers. If they question why some people have so much money while others have so little in this world, then let them inquire about that as well. Questions of money are often questions of social justice: the rich get richer, and the poor get poorer.

THE SPACE BETWEEN DIRECT INSTRUCTION AND INQUIRY

There is a scenario where, after eight or nine years of being spoon-fed worksheets and a steady diet of familiar problem sets after being shown several worked examples, our students are paralyzed in the face of the just-discussed problem. Not having been asked to inquire, they will not know how to inquire. These students often reach their high school years afraid of the unfamiliar problems and expecting constant and immediate closure to any mathematical uncertainty they may have. This disabled state comes from having a low image as a mathematical learner and thinker. Sit, wait, and you will be told how to get the right answer. Sit, wait, and you will be told how to do well on the test.

A continuum between direct instruction and inquiry could look like this: On the one hand, we have students working independently on problems, and on the other, we have teachers giving direct instruction (see figure 5.1). How much time do you spend on either extreme, and how much time do you spend in the middle? Both scenarios are extreme, with one end, where students are left to flounder, and the other, where they have no agency and take very little action. Having considered the extremes, we can now contemplate the vast middle, where most teachers live on most days.

Teachers decide how and when to give full instructional guidance during problems and tasks. Teachers make the moment-by-moment pedagogical decisions in any given chunk of instructional time. In any instructional period, we might go back and forth between individual and whole-group and small-group instruction several times. A lesson might happen on the blackboard. Some examples might be shown. Students might also share their own solutions with the whole group or with a student beside them.

Consider that your instructional goal is to get your students to generalize in terms of the -nth term of a linear sequence. You have looked at several patterns of various kinds with pattern blocks, toothpicks, and cubes. You might begin your class by asking your students to make a pattern that they know grows in a linear way. After ten or fifteen minutes, you might come together as a whole group and share some ideas. You could use your whiteboard or blackboard to write out the first terms in a pattern, say, 1, 2, 5, 14. You might draw out a t-table to look at how the pattern grows, noticing that multiples of 3 are added on each time. You could guide your students to see that the pattern grows very quickly but not by a nice and even multiple. You might encourage them to think of a function machine that takes the term before and performs two operations to get the next term. The explicit teacher move here is to show them why it is a "3n − 1" function and what that means.

How Much Guidance Should We Give? When?

Fully Guided Instruction ⟵——————————————⟶ Unguided Instruction

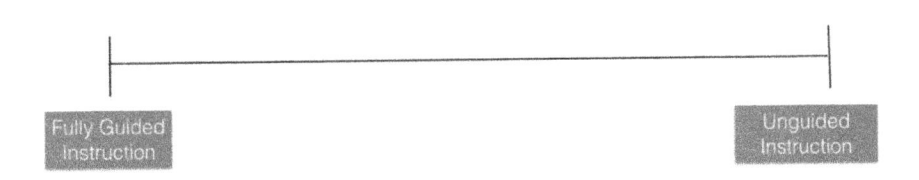

Figure 5.1.

This minilesson might take fifteen minutes. After that, you could set your students back to work, creating a new pattern and representing it in terms of n. This might take fifteen more minutes, leaving the last quarter of the class to come together, talk about and share student patterns. You do not need to hold the stage for long periods of time, but you do need to know when that timely burst of direct instruction would be helpful. Knowing when to give guidance and when to stand aside and watch is a key teacher skill in problem-solving classrooms.

FULL INSTRUCTIONAL GUIDANCE IN PROBLEM-SOLVING CLASSROOMS

I previously referred to a paper by Kirschner, Sweller, and Clark (2006) that speaks strongly against what the authors consider "minimally guided instruction," which they note has variously been called inquiry-based learning, project-based learning, or discovery learning. The authors pitted the minimally guided condition against their definition of *direct instructional guidance* and found that direct instructional guidance is far superior.

Full instructional guidance is a necessary condition for learning mathematics, but so much hinges on our own definitions of *direct instruction* and *guidance*. There are scripted mathematics programs out there that provide full scaffolding to students but take away the problematic nature of mathematics. There are definitions of direct instruction that only include whole-class, front-of-room instruction. There are also more inclusive definitions of *direct instruction* that include small-group instruction or individual feedback.

Instructional guidance does not have to be used exclusively at the start of a math period or at the beginning of a unit or sequence of instruction. It need not, and in many cases should not, take up large chunks of class time. Students can and must take action, making sense of topics and ideas for themselves, in problem-solving classrooms. Direct instruction can very effectively follow an exploration or guided investigation into a mathematical topic or idea. Indeed, this is probably the best time for direct instruction, when it is time for collective sense making, building understanding, and leaving the class for the day unpuzzled after exploring an interesting problem.

Full instructional guidance is designed by teachers, who decide when, how, and how much direct instruction to give. It is not didactic or overbearing, and it does not take space away from students' own thinking. More direct instructional guidance might be necessary when it is time to consolidate a conceptual base into a procedure, formula, or algorithm, for example. Less instructional guidance should often be given at the beginning of a mathematics period, as we want to activate our students' curiosity, puzzlement, and sense of wonder. If we want our students to be active inquirers into mathematics, then they need time and space to do it.

As previously noted, teachers are constantly directing an iterative back-and-forth pedagogical interplay between procedural and conceptual instruction. The same principle holds true for inquiry and direct instruction. Any given chunk of mathematics instructional time will probably have a back and forth in that time between procedures and concepts. Perhaps a one-hour instructional period could look like this:

- Explore a problem individually (ten minutes).
- Teacher notices a widespread misconception and gives a lesson to correct the course (five minutes).
- Back to work on the problem (fifteen minutes).
- Paired sharing of solutions (ten minutes).
- Whole-group discussion of math concepts (ten minutes).
- Follow-up problems or a quick "exit ticket" for students to explain what they have learned in a sentence or two (five to ten minutes).

Each given instructional period is unique and might break down differently. Teachers decide how best to use the time based on the needs of their students. Each period probably includes at least some whole-class instruction and explanation; some time for individual, paired, or group work; and some time for consolidation of concepts and feedback.

THE RIGHT AMOUNT OF INSTRUCTIONAL GUIDANCE AT THE RIGHT TIME

How much instructional guidance to give and when is the endlessly debatable question at the heart of deliberations over how best to teach mathematics. Instructional time is a finite, precious resource, and how we spend the bulk of our time in our mathematics classrooms is an important decision. On the one hand, we might have a classroom where full instructional guidance is given at all times. This class could be characterized by an in-depth explanation of the topic to be worked on, a handful of worked examples, and practice work. At the risk of sounding sarcastic, this instructional condition is often a continuous cycle: give homework, take up homework, work some new examples on the black- or whiteboard, repeat. If this was your school experience, then you are not alone.

In this instructional condition, we sometimes find skilled explainers of mathematics who are spellbinding and thorough in their explanations of powerful concepts. We find appropriate scaffolding and careful attention to cognitive load. Teachers do not to overwhelm students and break concepts down into their components accordingly. In this instructional condition, we might also find a monotonous state of tedium created by an unbroken rhythm of "drill and kill." Students in this instructional condition often communicate with their teacher only through marked work and taken-up homework. The quality of explanation in more traditional direct-instruction classrooms varies widely, as it of course does in all classrooms.

Consider how you would teach the relationship between circumference and diameter in any circle, which we know to be pi. There are choices to be made, pedagogical moves to make. Here is one possible instructional path:

1. Define *pi* as the relationship between circumference and diameter.
2. Show the formula: circumference = pi × diameter.
3. Explain that pi is an irrational number with an infinite number of digits.
4. Work through a few examples of how to use the formula for circles of different diameters with different-sized circles carefully sketched on the black- or whiteboard.
5. Give a problem set requiring students to work through basic examples of the formula, with a few wrinkles, variations, or contexts given at the end. (Solving for the diameter when the circumference is given, for example).

There is no ambiguity allowed here. The careful scaffolding given by this teacher leads students to know and use the formula. If the instructional goal is to know the meaning of *pi* and to apply it to find the circumference, then this sequence will be very successful. Direct instruction of this kind leads to worked examples, followed by what we might call "work" or "problems" in the sense of "mathematics questions to be completed."

The question is, Is this way more interesting than playing with different sizes of circles and noticing relationships? Pi exists. It is there to be found. We can guide our students to find it. No, they will not "discover" pi for the first time; that happened a long time ago. They will, however, be discovering pi for the first time for *them*.

The opposite instructional condition to the one described above is one where students are left to "find" or "discover" and make sense of important mathematics on their own. In this instructional condition, students might engage with a problem about some area of mathematics and work through the problem with little guidance given. In this condition, some students will have powerful "a-ha" moments, but many will not. Teacher guidance is needed. With careful teacher guidance, students can arrive at an understanding of the important concepts and big ideas of the mathematics at play, in this case the relationship between the circumference and diameter of any circle. In this instructional condition, students are encouraged to "discover" pi as if for the first time, which of course it is for them! Pi has been "discovered" multiple times in different cultures, and our uses for and precision with pi has improved over the past several thousand years. This should not stop our students from discovering pi for themselves, which they can do through carefully designed investigations. Give students a piece of string, a measuring tape or ruler, and a bunch of different-sized cylinders or can lids. Have them compare the circumferences of each circle to their diameters. Ask them what they notice. Point them in the right direction when they need it. Here is one possible instructional path through this investigation:

1. Tell students they will be investigating the characteristics of circles and the relationships that are found in circles.
2. Give a variety of string, can lids, and measuring tapes.
3. Instruct students to find the distance all the way around each circle using the string, which can be later laid against the measuring tape. Tell them that the word for perimeter of a circle is *circumference*.
4. Find the diameter of each circle and record these measurements.
5. Record all results. Ask students if they notice any mathematical relationships in each circle between the two measurements.
6. Notice if students consider using division; give prompting to use this operation if needed. (They may not think of *relationship* as having to do with a specific operation, or they may try to use addition or subtraction.)
7. Discuss the results. (You might find they have many results clustered around 3 after carrying out their division or perhaps around 3.1, depending on how precisely they measured.)
8. "Pull back the curtain." Explain the reason the results are clustered around 3.1. Given how popular March's Pi Day has become, they will probably know a few things about pi already.
9. Now show them how to work the formula: $C = \pi \times d$.
10. Give them a few examples to try.

The effectiveness of this instructional path depends on a full teacher explanation of the big reveal: Pi is the relationship between circumference and diameter. Students left to discover mathematical concepts on their own will be lucky to find anything at all. Full instructional guidance must be given, and here it is given at the end of the instructional sequence. This instructional sequence is effective because it builds curiosity, and it builds toward a goal. It is effective because it requires teachers to take action in the beginning to construct their understanding. This instructional path is about the thrill of thinking and finding a new and interesting relationship between two seemingly unrelated measurements (circumference and diameter).

Exploration of a mathematical topic combined with full instructional guidance at every step of the way and feedback leads to a robust understanding of the topic at hand. In this case, students should really get a feel for the number we call *pi*. They will come to know pi firsthand through their own investigation.

Misunderstandings about this more learner-centered style of instruction often focus on the idea that students are left alone to construct their own individual understanding of a math topic. Transmission of knowledge about pi from teacher to student is an easier and more efficient instructional path, but actively engaging with the concept is more interesting. If we see our students as empty vessels, then we can just pour the knowledge in. Brains are not containers, however. They can never be full, and they are not made to be filled.

Students, as novices in the art of mathematical thinking, need guidance at every step along the way. Skilled teachers in this more open instructional condition do not let their students flounder; they know the optimal amount of time to let students struggle, and they know the difference between productive and unproductive struggle. They function more like coaches, giving feedback and advice and watching for students who are not getting it. Productive struggle is characterized by actively exploring and working on a problem, choosing strategies, monitoring progress toward the goal (coming up with a result), and having a dynamic mind-set to solve the problem. Unproductive struggle occurs when a student cannot find a way into the problem. They can find no way to start, or their mathematical tool kit is not up to the task, or they misunderstand or do not understand at all the mathematics at play in the problem. Teachers of this second student do them no favors without some direct instruction or coaching.

DIRECT INSTRUCTION IN PROBLEM-SOLVING CLASSROOMS

For constructivist or inquiry-minded mathematics teachers, direct instruction has been given a bad reputation for creating closed-off, unthinking classrooms. However, a more traditional-minded teacher would see the inquiry condition as detrimental to learning. So much hinges on how we define *direct instruction*. Direct instruction is not a scripted program, taking every student through a step-by-step process toward the same goal at the exact same time. Direct instruction is not relentless lecturing through board work, with students dutifully copying the worked examples and the teacher's thoughts. Direct instruction is giving the right guidance, in the right way, at the right time, to the right student. It need not be whole-class instruction, although knowing when the whole class would benefit from clearing up a misconception together or looking at an idea or example is a key pedagogical decision.

Calling the class together for a deliberate five- to ten-minute burst of direct instruction is often necessary. Consider this a course correction or a furthering of their thinking.

All educators must make up their own minds. There are very personal choices to be made based on one's own strengths as a teacher, the strengths and weaknesses of the students, and the type of math being taught. As a general rule of thumb, there are very few math concepts that cannot be introduced in an intriguing and interesting way in kindergarten to high school classrooms.

Many big ideas in mathematics can be introduced through simple and interesting investigations by giving intriguing visuals or problems. The Pythagorean relationship, pi, integers, fraction operations—all can be opened up as mathematical ideas through powerful and interesting problems, tasks, or investigations. We inquire into these big mathematical ideas, we open them up as objects of our thought, and we start to build our understanding of them through purposeful work. Of course, good investigations are nothing without powerful teacher talk—deciding when to intervene, when to give whole-class instruction, and how to consolidate the activities. Students should never be left to just "discover" math on their own. Teachers have an important role to play in constructing understanding of powerful math concepts. Our students need us.

Each teacher has a different optimal balance, and even this can vary from day to day, from week to week, and from year to year. Some years your class will be more suited to exploring more or will need more direct instruction, and that's fine. Professionals need to know their own strengths and weaknesses and teach to their strengths while tempering their weaknesses. Classroom practice is a daily grind. Know yourself, educator, and know your students. Make purposeful instructional choices. Explore powerful and interesting mathematical ideas with your kids. Don't be afraid to explain concepts to them when they need it. There is no one "best practice"—there are better and worse practices. More importantly, there are better and worse practices for *you*.

ON DELIBERATE AND PURPOSEFUL PRACTICE

> Deliberate practice involves more than just repetition; it requires activities that are designed to improve performance, challenge the learner and provide feedback.—Marzano (2010)

The role of practice in problem-solving classrooms must be considered. We do our students no favors when we do not give them enough practice work. You need to do enough mathematics to be good at mathematics. Room must be made in problem-solving classrooms for skill and concept practice. Nobody questions a basketball player who spends hours practicing jump shots. We know baseball players take thousands of reps in the batting cage to get their swings just right. We need to make sure our students practice enough with mathematical concepts and skills. Our students need to put their skills into action.

As Daniel Pink says in his book *Drive*, we learn best when we have autonomy, mastery, and purpose. Problem-solving classrooms provide autonomy and purpose. Mastery is a powerful thing that comes with consolidation of skills and concepts over time through deliberate and purposeful practice. We need to do enough mathematics to get good at mathematics. The role of practice in problem-solving classrooms shouldn't be downplayed. It is through practice that we synthesize and connect mathematical skills and ideas. Here is what a progression to mastery of integer addition and subtraction might look like:

- Considering many contexts for when we use integers (temperature, sea level, golf, debt, for example). Harvesting all prior knowledge your students have about a subject is good practice in any grade and for any subject.
- Playing with number lines and colored tiles and developing a strong sense of integers as equal and opposite quantities from zero. Number lines are a powerful visual and spatial model for integers. Using two colors to show positive and negative quantities (for example, red and yellow) is a powerful way to make tangible something that seems intangible: negative numbers.
- Considering that opposite positive and negative integers sum to zero (the powerful zero principle). This can be shown with both the tile and the number-line model.
- Playing with addition and subtraction using colored tiles and number lines. Figuring out how they work. Conjuring "zero pairs" of tiles out of nowhere to make subtraction work. (That you can add in an infinite number of pairs of +1 and −1 is a powerful and massive idea that tends to blow students' minds.)
- Developing "rules" for addition and subtraction. Addition is combining or putting things together. For example, adding −7 and +5 results in more negative 1s, so the result must be negative. It is also appropriate now to look at how addition and subtraction are opposite operations and to look at ways to make subtraction more manageable.
- Practicing adding and subtracting integers now that we know what it all means.

In this last phase, students need time to practice adding and subtracting various expressions. They need time for the concepts to fit together. This will take different amounts of time, depending on the student. For example, one student might be given twenty expressions, and she might add or subtract them all accurately. Another student might only need ten expressions before you see that she gets it. Others still might need reteaching of the concept or an alternate conceptual path. Some will need feedback and more instruction. In any given lesson, some kids will be ready to consolidate their understanding and move on, while others will need more opportunities for practice. The amount of practice work needed will vary from student to student.

Concepts and procedures consolidate into doing the operation. They become forever intertwined, like a thick braid of rope, never to be pulled apart again. This rope represents the powerful state called *understanding*. We understand what integers are (the set of all positive and negative numbers and zero), and we can use them. The earlier scaffolding provided by the colored tiles and number lines tends to fall away as students become fluent with integer addition and subtraction. For some, the concrete and visual scaffolding may need to stay up for longer.

The right amount of practice at the right time is very important. Giving endless practice questions to those who are not ready is a recipe for defeat. Giving the right amount of practice at the right time brings a sense of mastery. This fulfilling and empowering sense of efficacy, that "I can do it" sense, is the end state we wish to reach. Practice should be deliberate, given for a reason, and given just in time for greatest effect. If I can't multiply yet, then don't give me twenty multiplication questions. Teach me the meaning of multiplication, and then show me how to multiply. Teach me. If I can multiply already, then do not give me fifty more questions. There is a "just right" amount of practice for all mathematical learners.

Consider this though: If you have lined up five order-of-operations worksheets, and you look around, and almost every kid is proficient after two worksheets, then why would you give three more? That is pointless busywork. Target the learners who need more support, and let the others try more interesting or complex problems, or put their skills to work in more interesting contexts on more complex problems.

Purposeful practice is practice that is thoughtful and deliberate while being responsive to individual students' needs. Students should have multiple and varied opportunities for practice. The right amount of practice at the right time increases confidence and mastery. Purposeful practice does not mean every student doing "numbers 1 to 72" on a worksheet at the exact same time. Giving the right task at the right time to the right student is what we should aim to do. Traditionally, we may have had all students doing the same practice work at the same time, regardless of individual readiness. This may once have looked like all students doing the same worksheet or textbook questions at the same time. Those who were ready to consolidate their understanding benefited, while those students who needed more support with the skills and concepts floundered. Purposeful practice strengthens the connection between skills, concepts, strategies, and thinking. It improves speed and accuracy and helps students to remember concepts, facts, and procedures. Within a problem-solving classroom, practice could be used to strengthen the understanding of mathematical concepts and big ideas introduced in tasks or to develop procedural and computational skill.

RESPONSIVE TEACHING IN MATHEMATICS CLASSROOMS

> The guide on the side is a poor pedagogue; or we don't want "a guide on the side" any more than we need a "sage on the stage." More proactive partnership will be required.—Michael Fullan (2013)

A "sage on the stage" is a skilled and spellbinding lecturer or storyteller, in the best-case scenario. In the worst, this "sage" is sagelike only in his or her mind and holds the stage for far too long while eyes begin to droop. At risk of tautological reasoning, we might say that good lecturing is good, and bad lecturing is bad. Sit for too long listening, and you will probably wish for and need to take action.

The "guide on the side" is probably too hands off, too aloof, not present enough for his or her students. The guide on the side is too passive. The guide on the side needs to get off the sidelines and start moving around the classroom, giving feedback when needed at just the right time, and guiding students along their own thinking pathways toward understanding.

A skilled pedagogue in a problem-solving classroom is probably more like a "coach in the middle." Coaches during games stay on the sidelines, but math class is not a game. It is something far less formal, far less of a show or event. Learning is much messier than four quarters of a game of basketball. Although timebound, it is much less constrained by rules and regulations, and it is not refereed. Teachers should not stay on the sidelines; they should be actively walking, talking, and interacting with their students. Instructional guidance must be given at the right time. Feedback must be given at the right time.

Math class is more like a basketball practice. One student might be shooting free throws, getting advice to keep her elbows in to shoot straight at the basket. Another might be working on an interesting problem on her own. A group of students might be off in the corner, working on a problem on a whiteboard or chart paper. A basketball coach, for example, might spend some time giving direct feedback to the whole team during a practice but probably spends a lot more time giving specific feedback to individuals (demonstrating floor spacing in a drill or correcting a player's form on a jump shot, for example) or to small groups (a center needs far different feedback than a point guard, as she spends most of her time closer to the basket). The coach steps in when needed with the appropriate explicit instruction at the right time. The coach gives feedback on an ongoing basis.

A coach during practice is always active, in the middle of things. Perhaps we might think of ourselves as more "in the middle" than on the sidelines. This new metaphor would also defuse one of the common arguments leveled at our system these days: that we simply just let kids go off to "discover" all that they will learn at their own pace and style. The ever-active coach is always talking, giving personalized feedback, and offering advice for how to improve.

The "coach in the middle" is a better pedagogue, in most circumstances, than the "sage on the stage" or the "guide on the side." Coaches in problem-solving classrooms know how and when to give full instructional guidance and when to step back and let independent practice happen. Coaches know how to give guidance and feedback at the right moment to the right student at the right time. Teachers know when to explain and when to step back and let students inquire into interesting ideas in mathematics. They know how to set their students going down the right instructional path. They manage instructional time and make the minute-by-minute decisions that are needed to move learning forward.

Chapter Six

Mathematics Classrooms Are Spaces for Talking, Reasoning, Thinking, and Wondering

> *Axiom: Mathematics classrooms are places of talking, thinking, conjecturing, and wondering about the mystery and beauty of mathematics.*

Mathematics is meant to be talked about. Mathematical objects are meant to be examined and played with. If students expect otherwise, then it is because they have been enculturated to expect mathematics classrooms to be different kinds of spaces: quiet places of solitary work with the only verbal interactions occurring between them and their teacher, and even then only when they deliberately seek out help.

Once I gave what I thought was an interesting problem, something that was going to make the students think. It was a problem to be thought about and discussed in pairs. It was going to cause them all to have sudden breakthroughs, "a-ha" moments that left them stunned and eager to share their results. Students dutifully worked through the problem and came up with some interesting results. At the end of the period, one student asked, "Can I just have a worksheet to do on my own next time?" This happens more than you might think. This student was signaling his sense of mastery with that one mode of learning, and to be fair, in this case, he had a great handle on the mathematics in the task. Many students associate worksheets with the doing of mathematics itself. For some students, worksheets *are* mathematics.

A worksheet has a clear beginning and end and is something you can just patiently (or not so patiently) chug through until you reach the end. You have closure when you are finished. You can put the worksheet away in a binder and forget about it. A lot of problems are much messier: their structure is initially murky until you engage with the problem, and it begins to reveal itself to you. After that happens, the pleasure of problem-solving hopefully kicks in: solving the problem in your own unique way with your own tools and strategies is its own kind of mastery.

Students in problem-solving classrooms can handle worksheets, although the opposite may not be true, and kids who just want the worksheet may be missing out on the beauty, wonder, and (frankly) interest of mathematics. As an educator, what would you say to the kid who says, "Just give me a worksheet next time"?

MATHEMATICS IS SOCIAL

The myth of the solitary mathematician persists in our culture. Imagine a mathematician at work: you might think of a man, possessed by a mad genius and inspired by a secret world that is his and his alone, frantically scribbling equations on a very large blackboard. This caricature about the doing of mathematics is internalized by our students and becomes part of their mental image of *doing mathematics*. Modern mathematics, in its turn, is more collaborative than ever before, with groups of people sharing their results on interesting problems using powerful technological tools and the tools of social media, like blogs and collaborative wikis, where results are shared, updated, discussed, and celebrated.

Students must be shown that mathematics classrooms are talking classrooms. They are places for sharing and collaborating. The more we speak of mathematics and about mathematics, the more we understand mathematics. The more we speak aloud in the language of mathematics, the more we will be able to harness this powerful thinking tool for our own use.

Mathematics classrooms can and should be powerful discursive spaces, with students using mathematical tools, symbols, images, and vocabulary in offering their powerful reasoning, conjectures, and wondering aloud about interesting problems. Talking classrooms are filled with mathematical discourse, day in, day out, using the powerful discipline-based tools, including words, symbols, and mental representations brought into being, to present and defend their ideas and reach conclusions. Mathematics classrooms should be places of talking, thinking, conjecturing, and wondering. They should be open spaces, always, for students to think mathematically about interesting problems and through open questions, tasks, and investigations. Students use their own powerful mathematical thinking to wonder, ask questions, explore their own reasoning about problems, and provide proof, convincing themselves and others of the truth of their solutions.

Talking in math classrooms should not be an event relegated to occasional "fun" classes. Mathematics classrooms can and should be powerfully social environments. Doing mathematics should be social. Finding a balance between paired or group and individual work is important, as is finding the right time to deliver those small-group or whole-class minilessons. Students should spend as much time talking to other students as they do to us. In math-talk classrooms, teachers constantly offer help; advice; feedback; and, most of all, intervention at the right time to push mathematical thinking forward.

Students will surprise us with the power of their thinking if we let them. Pedagogical surprise is near-constant in problem-solving classrooms. On our thinking journeys together, we explore new and divergent paths to solutions, learning from each other as we go. Teachers in problem-solving classrooms are responsive to student thinking and willing to follow new courses of action, new lines of thinking and attack on problems, and new representations. There is no single path to the goal in problem-solving classrooms.

SILENCE, PLEASE—IT'S MATH CLASS

When I first started out as a teacher, I sometimes covered for an experienced math teacher with many years of service to the school and board. She was very good at what she did, and what she did was teach mathematics in what we might describe as a "traditional" way. Her classroom was an example of skilled traditional teaching based on routine; worked examples; and full explanation of facts, procedures, and concepts every single step of the way. Homework was taken up and marked every day, lessons were given in the form of worked examples on the blackboard, and students were set back to work again.

Mathematical discourse was missing from this classroom. Talking was missing from this classroom. Students never talked except to ask for help. They expected the classroom to always be a silent working space. I was brand new and terrified of getting in trouble for letting her kids talk. I faithfully tried to teach her way because that's what I thought I was supposed to do. I was afraid of the disapproving looks and words from my colleagues. But something felt off, and the students probably felt it, too. You could see that some students were just about bursting at the seams, wanting to talk about the more interesting problems in their problem sets, but this was not part of their learning culture.

We are better served by talking about mathematical ideas. We learn to teach, in part, through how we were taught. We tend to reproduce the conditions in which we ourselves learned. When I first starting teaching, I didn't know that math classrooms could (and should) be talking classrooms. I saw them as quiet spaces, where you should hear a pin drop, and students silently approached the teacher's desk to ask questions if and only if they had a question. Otherwise, they did not speak. We were marked on our work at certain teacher-decided points in time, usually on quizzes in the middle of a unit, and then again at the end of the unit. For the most part, that's all the feedback we got unless we asked for help. Then, we made our corrections and moved on to the next topic. Repeat this sequence for ten months at a time.

Thinking was something that happened in kids' heads and wasn't shared except on tests. The textbook decided the next day's lesson. Thinking was a written artifact on a page at the end of a unit. This is the way I was taught to teach math, in lockstep, unending procession, jumping from textbook section to textbook section.

A SILENT KID SPEAKS

If students are not taught how to use the language of mathematics in service of classroom discourse, then they will not know how to use the language of mathematics in speaking to each other. Talking changes everything, and when kids start to talk in the math classroom, they don't stop. They will talk about the problem they are working on with others. They will come in the next day still talking about the previous day's work. They will come in eager to talk about prime numbers or videos about math topics they saw on YouTube. They will wonder aloud about things like infinity and whether pi never ends. Mathematics will be more fully integrated into their lives and not just something that they use inside the four walls of their classrooms and leave behind when they walk out of the school doors for the last time.

Talking spaces are spaces for wondering aloud about interesting mathematical ideas. Our classrooms are those wondering spaces, those talking spaces. We are used to thinking about voice in the writing classroom. How about in the math classroom? Are we as teachers ready to hear students' own original and unique mathematical voices as they talk and reason their ways through interesting mathematical problems and ideas?

Sometimes that quiet student hiding in the corner, who only speaks when spoken to and who doesn't usually engage in math class, will find a sudden spark of insight into a problem and excitedly share her solution. Or it could be that kid who does not do well on pencil-and-paper assessments but comes alive when he is given the chance to reason aloud in collaborative work with his peers.

An eighth-grade class once tackled this relatively simple, classic problem structure posed by Dan Meyer (in a task he called "Dueling Discounts") and others involving reasoning about percent and percent discounts: *What is better: 20 percent off or $20 off?* It is an interesting task of the "which scenario is better, when" class. You could pose the problem for 10 percent or for any other percent with similar results. The key idea is that there is a tipping point at which it is always better to take the straight discount. At this tipping or hinge point, our understanding of the mathematics of the problem is flipped over. A guess-and-check attack strategy might not lead students quite as far as they need to get, which is the hinge point. A full proof, a full line of reasoning, would show that, at exactly $100, you get $20 off in both cases. At $101 dollars, the 20% discount gives you $20.20 off, and the discount only gets better from there.

A boy once sprang to life in collaborative group work on this problem. He knew the answer, he just *saw* the answer, and words spilled out of him as he excitedly shared his reasoning with his peers. He enthusiastically led his group through his reasoning and confidently explained his mathematical thinking. The teacher said, "He never talks in math class." She noted that he was also on an individual education plan at the time and often had trouble explaining his thinking on paper. Given the chance to reason out loud, to use his own words, he stunned her with his powerful reasoning. She was surprised, and he was surprised. Feeling successful in math class was not his usual daily lived reality. This story is not unique. It happens all the time in problem-solving classrooms. You might call it "mathematical surprise." No matter how much we prepare our lessons, anticipate possible outcomes, and truly and deeply "know the math" in the tasks we use, students will always surprise us with the power of their thinking. It's what we do with that surprise that matters.

Over the course of years, I gradually came to open up my mathematical teaching practices. Not coincidentally, this happened when I really started to know and understand the mathematical content knowledge in the curriculum, as well as how best to teach it. I started to assess more and test less—and, finally, to not test at all. The sky didn't fall, and I didn't have angry parents on the phone or at the door. Nobody asked me, "Where's the tests?" I developed a problem-solving approach to teaching math and started letting kids talk to each other. I switched the default from not talking to usually talking, and our classroom became an open thinking space; an idea space; and a space for actively moving, sharing, and engaging with big mathematical ideas.

Students started to like math class. There were no more audible groans from eighth-graders as I desperately tried to get them excited about one problem or another. I didn't have to do the "Pythagorean dance" any more, begging and pleading for them to find relevance and interest in ancient formulae, rules, and algorithms. They no longer needed to be cajoled or coerced into talking about their work, and they weren't secretive about their work, hiding it from view, covering it defensively with their arms as I walked by. In Dr. Cathy Bruce's (2007) words, "math is . . . a social endeavor . . . where thinking, talking, agreeing, and disagreeing are encouraged" (1). At least it should be! We make our thinking visible to others when we share our ideas with others, and the teacher's job of assessing her students is made much easier.

Talking changes everything in mathematics classrooms. Once math classrooms become talking classrooms, they become thinking classrooms, and thinking is contagious. Talking and thinking won't stop, ideas will flow and be shared, and our job of assessing student thinking and understanding becomes much easier. In my experience, our classroom became a much more open, interesting, creative, and collaborative space when it became an open space for thinking and talking. We wondered together about the big ideas in math, scrawling solutions on chart paper, justifying our reasoning as we went, and building our understanding of big mathematical concepts together.

If we are open to creating a culture of math talk and truly value student voice in the math classroom—starting from the very first day, the very first class—then we will be amazed at the culture that develops. Consider this decision, one that teachers confront at the beginning of each school year: how to start the very first class. Do we start with running through lists of rules and regulations or giving review worksheets? Try picking an interesting first-day problem instead. Pick one that you know will get your students talking and thinking on the very first day of class. One that many teachers find successful is the classic problem about doubling pennies. Would you rather I give you $1,000,000 now, or would you rather I give you one penny today, giving you double that amount for each day that follows, for a whole month? This problem gets students thinking about the power of doubling and about exponential growth. It has a surprising result, and it is open to different problem-solving techniques, methods, and representations. It is accessible, not too wordy, and gets at a very large mathematical idea: that compounding money is a powerful force, and exponentiation makes numbers grow very quickly. It disrupts their intuition about number, as humans are very bad at thinking in terms of exponential growth. Around the middle of the month, if you choose the pennies, you only have a handful of dollars. How is it that turns into over ten million dollars by the end of the month? That seems impossible, but that is the mystery of mathematics. Mathematics is mysterious, and our intuition about it is sometimes fallible. Pick a big and wide problem like this for the first day of class, and watch a problem-solving culture flourish.

Try not to regulate their talk too much while they work. Let them see that a mathematics classroom is a place where ideas are shared and talked about. Share solutions at the end of class. Celebrate the beginning of a new and open math culture for a new school year. Starting the first day of class with a thought-provoking problem without formal talking structures will make developing these formal structures much easier.

A math class culture where students know they are expected to speak is an empowering one. When students learn to interact with each other in a math talk culture, they will surprise us with how articulate, passionate, and well-reasoned they can be about mathematics. In this culture, students will constantly surprise us with the raw power of their mathematical thought, of their interesting, individual, and creative mathematical reasoning.

In talking classrooms, mathematical ideas, strategies, and solutions are not kept secret. Sharing is the norm, and rooms are constantly abuzz with mathematical argument, with the delightful sounds of learning:

- "Here's what I'm thinking."
- "Can you see why I'm right?"
- "I think you're wrong because your numbers don't add up."
- "What strategy should we try?"
- "Have you thought about _____?"

There are many lists of "math talk moves," talk routines, and ways to get students talking in math class out there, but regardless of which formal protocols or prompts you use to get students talking, give them lots of chances to practice talking to each other in ways that are accountable to themselves, to the culture of the classroom, and to mathematics itself.

Students can be taught to revoice each other's mathematical arguments, to add on to their thinking, and to ask questions to push and probe for further thought. Sometimes the simplest and best talk move can be just to let students talk it out—give them an interesting problem, and let them talk about it. Regardless of how you get your students talking, once you build a culture of talking, your classroom will be alive with powerful mathematics talk.

ASSESSMENT AND EVALUATION IN PROBLEM-SOLVING CLASSROOMS

Assessment is the constant process of judgment and discernment used by teachers about student learning. Evaluation, usually quantitative, of the quality of our students' work serves our grading systems. Assessment is not just something that happens between a teacher and what a student has written on paper. Assessment is something much more than just a piece of paper with a grade and perhaps some feedback passed back and forth between teacher and student. Assessment is more process than product. Pencil-and-paper products only tell part of the story and often are only a small piece of the story of a student's learning.

Learning is not something to be kept secret, and understanding is not something only checked at certain set intervals. In problem-solving classrooms, you will always know where your students are in their mathematical understanding because you will *hear* them, and they will *tell* you. If their written work shows some misconceptions, then you question those misconceptions by asking for clarification. If you are unsure of what they are thinking in a piece of written work or their steps are unclear, then you ask them rather than just mark them wrong.

Teachers learn through experience some common and frequent mistakes that students make and how to address them. Students will often tell you that, for example, 1/2 + 3/4 = 4/6. Why? They have added the numerators and added the denominators because that is how they think adding always works. They don't understand yet how the notation for fractions works, or they need more work on representing fractions with concrete materials. If enough students make this mistake, then it is a good time to do a whole-class minilesson. Talking to the student who has made this error is the best way to diagnose the problem, much like a doctor does with her patients. It is not about right and wrong answers in the end. It's about understanding. It is about improvement over time. Teachers guide students along the path of improvement every single day.

Feedback is most helpful when it is frequent and specific and targeted to specific misconceptions. Feedback does not occur at the end of an instructional cycle or unit, when it can no longer be used. Feedback is given throughout the instructional cycle. In talking classrooms, feedback happens constantly, day in and day out. Understanding is constantly monitored. Students don't need to wait until they get their tests back to figure out how they're doing. They are always acting on their feedback, monitoring their own understanding, speaking in their own voices, and asking for help when they don't get it.

THE MYSTIQUE OF THE MATH TEST

As noted by Wiggins and McTighe (1998), teachers are used to using tests as the mark and measure of student achievement. Using tests is a long-standing habit. Test mystique—the idea that tests are the best, most objective, and pure measure of student achievement—still prevails in mathematics classrooms perhaps more than in any other subject. Typically, we decide on the set of test items that we believe best represents the current unit of study and give this set of items to students at the end of a learning cycle or unit.

Test mystique, to use Bennett, Dworet, and Weber's (2008) term, is persistent and pervasive in our dealings with our students, as tests are sometimes seen to have a "mystical capacity to open a window into a student's inner being and the workings of his or her mind," and teachers often "defer to test results even when those results contradict their own observations and conclusions arrived at over months of on-site observations and analyses." Student work quality as seen on one piece of work or completed in one class period is presumed to be more valid than weeks or even months of daily class work with attendant teacher observations, assessment checkpoints, checks for understanding along the learning journey.

Tests are presumed to be objective and somehow more valid than our own conversations and observations with students we interact with every single day. Some teachers are reluctant to trust their own informed judgments and classroom assessments, deferring instead to testing results—many of them standardized—for the final word about the strengths and needs of their own students. A single pencil-and-paper measure must not override our judgment. Tests are time efficient but often do not provide the best assessment of our students' knowledge and understanding of mathematics concepts. In problem-solving classrooms, we need to trust our eyes and ears most of all.

When I stopped giving math tests, I felt I knew my students so much better. Short quizzes were used only to check in on basic skills—for example, adding and subtracting integers correctly. The unit test becomes unnecessary when you know your students well from daily interactions with them. You do not need to put together a grab bag full of questions about various topics and concepts to assess their knowledge and thinking.

All mathematics teachers should come to develop their own personal assessment principles informed by beliefs, awareness of our own strengths, and our own pedagogical methods. Here are some possible assessment principles for problem-solving mathematics classrooms:

1. Engage students in purposeful talk about what they are learning as they work on a classroom task. Talking to students is a valuable assessment tool. Record and use tracking sheets with anecdotes from this purposeful talk, and treat it as valuable data—part of the bigger picture of how and what the student is learning.
2. Do not feel you must evaluate your students by giving a test. Most of us are taught that we are supposed to give tests. Consider other methods, like performance tasks or interviews.
3. Develop a system to document observations and anecdotes from conversations. It is often hard to stop in the flow and write things down, but techniques like using checklists will help. I have experimented with using tape recorders (old school) and now apps to record observations. In the era of ubiquitous mobile phones, documenting student work has never been easier. Remember the power of the camera roll; take pictures of work in progress frequently.
4. Use frequent checkpoints when teaching new concepts. This relates to the concept of chunking. Allow students to check in frequently in their learning. Give students checklists, which will aid in task completion. Give frequent, short, low-stakes assessments to check in with student thinking, catch their misconceptions, and help them develop a full

understanding of the mathematical concept or ideas. Talk to or conference with your students frequently as they work on longer problems or assessments.
5. Give frequent feedback to improve student learning. A state of helplessness often sets in when a student does not know if he or she is doing the work "right"; feedback helps to redirect a student positively, and giving feedback helps to bring a task closer to completion.

Black and William (1998), in their important work on feedback in the assessment process, point out that a single piece of directed feedback is sometimes all it takes to move learning forward. One good piece of actionable feedback is worth more than most other assessment methods. Feedback moves learning forward.
6. Trust your own judgment! You know your students best. You know the curriculum, and you have created the classroom culture. Trust your own assessment choices and methods.

ASSESSMENT IS "SITTING BESIDE"

According to Evangeline Harris Stefanakis (2002), "The word *assess* comes from the Latin *assidere*, which means *to sit beside*. Literally then, *to assess* means to *sit beside the learner*." Teachers all have powerful stories of "sitting beside." Although we often don't have time on a daily basis to sit beside every student, when we do, we learn so much about them. Possibly their conversation with you lays bare a misconception they have about a concept. It could be that they make a breakthrough on a mathematical topic, a sudden "a-ha" moment, right as they are talking to you. You might be able to identify a strategy that will help them move their thinking forward.

Here is a story of "sitting beside." A student was struggling with his multiplication chart. He was attempting to fill in the 10×10 grid with his multiplication facts. He made skip-counting errors in the 3 and 7 columns. He had an empty box in the middle where the commonly forgotten or tricky facts are—such as 8×7, and 9×7. Consider what you might have said to him if you were sitting beside him. Which questions would you ask to tease out what he knows about multiplication or what he is struggling with? Was it simply errors he was making with counting near the top of the chart, or did he misunderstand something deeper and larger about multiplication? Which times table facts is this student comfortable with? Which ones are sticky? Which ones does he have committed to his long-term memory? What will you do next to help him? Sitting beside him and having a conversation allows you to access his thinking, and you, as the teacher, can plan a course of action to help him.

"Sitting beside" can be more or less formal as needed for each student. Some students may not need it at all. You could schedule more formal conferences or check-ins with your students who need more. Seek out those students who have passed the point of productive struggle in their work or who are so far off track that they would benefit from your guidance in that moment. "Just in time" feedback, or course correction, is often what is needed for our learners.

As you move around the classroom monitoring, listening, and watching, here are some questions that might run through your own head:

- Who is struggling? Why are they struggling?
- Which misconceptions are evident in her work?
- Which feedback would help him get past the feeling of being stuck?
- Who is still in a state of productively struggling (in the flow of problem-solving) and should be left alone?
- Who has reached or is near the giving-up point, where productive struggle has turned to frustration? What will I do to move those students' learning forward?

Assessment is less about guesswork when you sit beside and have a conversation than it is about having a real and human conversation. You become aware of each student's understandings and their misunderstandings, and best of all you do not need to wait until later to mark a piece of work to get that picture of their learning. Feedback cycles should be kept tight and short. Frequent feedback is necessary for all of us to learn. That is not to say you will be able to "sit beside" everyone every single day. But you will likely only need to target certain students on certain days, when they need it. Assessment should be more of an ongoing conversation than a series of numbers in a grade book.

Tests, if you use them, should confirm what you already know about your learners. You have checked in with them frequently, and you know where they are in their learning and what they need to move their thinking forward. We need theories of assessment that are simple to understand and based on the shared humanity of teachers and learners. We need to focus on the learners in front of us and see assessment as a human act, a metaphorical or literal "sitting beside." You will not be able to sit beside everyone today, but perhaps you don't need to. Pick one to three kids, and make time to sit beside them and talk to them about what they are working on. Record what they say, but talk to them most of all. Want to know what your students are thinking? Just ask them. Assessment is a conversation. It is an ongoing dialogue of shared learning between teacher and student that happens daily and is only finished when the year or course is over.

Chapter 6
REASONING, PROVING, AND JUSTIFYING

Reasoning involves developing ideas, making mathematical conjectures, justifying results, and using evidence. Reasoning, proving, justifying—these are actions that are well suited to problem-solving classrooms, and they are particularly well suited to math-talk classrooms, where reasoning is heard out loud as often as it is seen on paper.

Students generally are not given enough chances to develop their own powerful lines of mathematical reasoning. They are not given enough chances to provide proof of their reasoning—lines of argument that convince themselves and others of the mathematical truth of their work. Students should be given lots of opportunities to develop and explain and justify their own mathematical reasoning. When we use our mathematical reasoning, it is because we know that mathematics is meant to be made sense of and understood.

Problem-solving classrooms, where students engage in authentic mathematical discourse, are places where mathematical reasoning comes to life. Some things that students should be doing as they develop their mathematical reasoning abilities include:

- learning to trust their own reasoning;
- learning to use their own reasoning to convince others of the truth and correctness of their results;
- proving results as true as they can for any given task or problem, whether that means generalizing for all cases or just for a few;
- justifying their estimates;
- making generalizations using algebra, for example, about a given linear pattern (e.g., you might notice that a toothpick pattern grows by three toothpicks each time, and therefore a multiplier of three must be in the algebraic expression for that pattern);
- choosing the best calculation tool for the problem they are working on, whether it is addition, subtraction, multiplication, division, or higher-powered tools, such as applying the order of operations, fraction or integer operations, or exponentiation in later grades; and
- constructing models for how things might work in the context of a given problem.

Our very young mathematicians are capable of reasoning their way through complex ideas about things like counting, patterns, geometric shapes, and numbers and operations. As they progress in mathematics and have more representational tools at their disposal, their reasoning becomes more abstract. Simply put, they are able to reason in more sophisticated ways as they progress. Our students become more confident in their abilities at bringing new mathematics into being, as they are given more chances to exercise their reasoning. The key thing is that our students are becoming more confident in their judgments as young mathematicians. We want them to be able to use their mathematical thinking tools to decide what's best or what's fair. We want them to justify their thinking. We want them always probing the mathematical world around them with their confident judgments.

We once took a picture of a bag of chips in a vending machine inside our school. The price was $1.50 for 32 grams. This bag of chips was just down the hall and offered a powerful opportunity for students to exercise their mathematical reasoning. The task was a picture of the bag with the price and the weight noted, with the following prompt: *What's a fair price?* Young children have their own powerful intuitive sense of what is fair; using mathematics to build on our intuition is much more powerful. Just try to split a cookie in an uneven way, for example. They will always call you on your unfairness. In this case, students offered numbers as precise as $0.29, based on their own research into the prices of potato chips, their own reasoning, and their own calculations. They concluded, through common sense backed up by mathematics, that this price for this tiny bag of chips was a really big rip-off. "What's best?" or "What's fair?" prompts are good for activating our students' reasoning. With their mathematical judgment, or discernment, thus activated, they must convince others of the truth of their mathematical argumentation.

CRITICAL THINKING AS MAKING SOUND MATHEMATICAL JUDGMENTS

Exercising mathematical judgment is what critical thinking looks like and sounds like in problem-solving mathematics classrooms. We use our mathematical judgment to make decisions about things that matter in the world. We use our mathematical judgment to help us decide what is better, what is best, and what is the best deal, to decide the best course of action for ourselves, given the calculations or mathematical decisions we have made.

Critical and creative thinking are not often considered as important parts of mathematics classrooms, but they should be. Critical and creative thinking are two sides of perhaps the same coin and are both adjacent to mathematical thinking. If the math process standards are the actions of doing math, then it makes sense then that these actions will, at times, encompass critical and creative thinking. Critical thinking is, at best, ill defined. The role of teachers in teaching critical thinking is debated, and indeed, it is debatable whether it can be taught. Thinking critically requires a good amount of domain-specific knowledge, in this case mathematics, in service of our common sense, our powers of judgment. An economical definition of *critical thinking: making sound judgments.* If we wanted to flesh out our definition a bit more for mathematics classrooms, then we could say, *making sound judgments about situations using the tools of mathematics.*

The best way to think critically is first to think. I risk circular logic there, but think about it: The best way to learn to think is to think. The best way to learn to think critically is to think critically. Worthwhile mathematical tasks, as discussed in chapter 1, will often give us the opportunity to think critically using mathematics.

Teachers in problem-solving classrooms understand that all students are capable of critical thinking. Mathematical knowledge and skill gained as children grow older allows them to think ever more critically. Critical thinking should not be thought of as higher-order thinking but rather a continued growth and development of the ability to make sound judgments about things that matter. Critical thinking in mathematics is not just for gifted learners; all students can develop their mathematical reasoning. Our young mathematicians will make judgments as they solve problems, decide which path to follow, revise their solution paths, and draw conclusions. They will pick the best representations for their mathematical work, and they will grow in confidence, the more opportunities they have to reason with the tools of mathematics.

One student, given a chance to develop his own mathematical model, decided to explore the projected career points totals of various hockey players. He built a model, projecting their career points totals, building in scoring averages, and accounting for injury and retirement age. Through his models, he assigned precise numbers: 989; 1,043; and 1,289. He presented his reasoning to his classmates. He reasoned with all available evidence to draw a conclusion, made choices about which information mattered, and came up with numbers. He exercised his critical judgment.

In the National Council for Teachers of Mathematics *Standards of Mathematical Practice*, there is the statement that students should "construct viable arguments and critique the reasoning of others." To do so requires a lot of modeling, structure, and practice, an entire process of learning how to trust their own reasoned opinions, results, and judgments.

The more opportunities our students are given to reason, to prove, the more confident they will be in their solutions as young mathematicians. We want them to be able to use their mathematical thinking tools to decide what's best or what's fair. We want them to justify their thinking. We want them always to probe the mathematical world around them with their confident judgments.

MAKE REASONING A DAILY ROUTINE

It is helpful to have repeatable talking routines that are short, powerful, and effective. They should be activities or tasks that are used regularly to promote talking, reasoning, and thinking. Sometimes all it takes is a picture or visual to activate our students' mathematical thinking. We should make reasoning a regular routine, daily if possible, to get kids talking and sharing their powerful thinking out loud. There are many repeatable reasoning routines you can use to get kids talking, thinking, justifying, and listening to the mathematical viewpoints of others.

Reasoning is more than just something we do on word problems. Reasoning is a part of the daily life of problem-solving mathematics classrooms. Proof, rigorous formal proof, is the realm of mathematicians, but proving answers, justifying results, and convincing ourselves and others of the truth of our work is the work of all of us.

Chapter Seven

Mathematics Can Be Playful

Axiom: Mathematics can, and should, be full of curiosity, creativity, and play.

Mathematics classrooms can and should be creative spaces for generating new and interesting mathematics and for playing with the big and powerful ideas of mathematics. Problem-solving classrooms are full of curiosity, with students constantly in a state of wonder about new and interesting mathematical ideas. Mathematics is meant to be played with; mathematical objects are not meant to sit and get dusty on mental shelves. Mathematical objects are meant to be taken out, played with, taken apart, and put back together again.

MATHEMATICS IS CREATIVE

If we as teachers do not see math as a generative process, a creative process, then we will not find creative thinking in our classrooms. Problem-solving classrooms will always have an element of creativity, unless we force our own methods, techniques, and processes on our students. It will always be our job to consolidate purposefully and to offer suggestions for more efficient or effective solutions. It will always be our job to help our students build their skills and to learn how to bring their mental representations into being. It is in the range and variety of the student work, with all its unique ways of thinking and entry points into mathematics problems and tasks, that we find creativity.

I consider critical thinking in mathematics classrooms in the previous chapter. We could distinguish creative and critical thinking by saying that one is about "making" while the other is about "assessing" or "judging." This is not a fixed binary, however; both are intrinsically tied together. Creative thinking is complementary to critical thinking and is a key component of problem-solving classrooms. One possible concise and precise definition of *creativity* is this: *making something new*. We could flesh out this definition for mathematics classrooms by saying: *Mathematical creativity is making something new with available mathematical tools, symbols, and representations.*

Making something new does not have to mean creating mathematics that has never existed in the world before. Mathematics builds on the foundation of what has come before, with certain time-tested techniques and methods, but if you are a student and you are doing a mathematical problem or task, then you are making something new and unique *to you* every single time. Problem-solving classrooms leave room for students to explore problems in their own ways.

To the painter, different types of paints, papers, brushes, or canvases are the tools. We can learn to paint, and once we know how to paint, our repertoire will expand, and we can truly make something new. To the mathematician, the mind is the canvas, and we have access to all our mental mathematical tools, representations, and models to bring our thoughts into being. The mathematics learner is learning how to make new things with this set of mental tools, representations, and associated calculations and lines of reasoning.

There is relatively little untutored creativity in the math classroom. In the math classroom, we are going to use our basic tool kit to help us "make something new." We need to know how to use the basic operations, and we need to build knowledge and skill with fractions, integers, and a number of other things. Along the way, our students can be shown that mathematics is a powerfully generative and creative process.

Creativity thrives under constraints. We must know where "the box" is and work "inside the box" so that we can later work "outside the box." Many mathematics problems have their own constraints, but in using those constraints, we can still come up with interesting and creative solutions to problems. Consider this problem, which you may have seen before and even used:

> Ten people meet for the first time. They all shake hands with each other to introduce themselves. How many handshakes will happen?

This problem has sparked many creative and interesting student solutions in classrooms worldwide. This problem inspires concrete modeling (actually shaking hands), interesting problem-solving paths, and sometimes interesting misconceptions to be considered along the way. This problem could be about combinations, patterning, or using the pigeonhole principle. Really, it is about finding a new way to count. We can work with kids to generalize the structure of this problem, depending on their age. We might have a specific curricular reason for using this problem. We might not—we might just be looking at our students' interesting ways of thinking about the problem.

Kids have subtle and interesting ways of thinking about problems. In working on interesting problems, hints of creativity come out. The transition from thinking mathematically to representing and explaining their thinking out loud often leads to some "magic." This is not pure, unfettered "splash the paint on the page," Jackson Pollock creativity here, but it is subtle and unique ways of thinking about the problem. Think of painters choosing different pigments or using slightly different shades of the same color. Students will choose the mathematical tools and representations that will help them to solve problems.

Once in a while, a student will come up with a radically divergent problem path, even one you have never seen before. This happens in problem-solving classrooms. A kid will have a "eureka" moment and see something in a new way. This is the "je ne sais quoi" moment of creativity, the magical moment of insight that happens when we, as is our human birthright, think deeply about interesting problems. If we are open to kids' thinking in math classrooms, then we will see and hear those subtle variations that we call creative thinking in the math classroom. We should all be open to it. A math problem is an empty canvas; give kids mathematical tools and skills, and see how they fill it.

Mathematics really doesn't get enough credit for its playfulness, its sense of fun, and its true mischievous spirit. Mathematics has a reputation for its cold and austere beauty, its aloofness, as G. H. Hardy said, but we can picture it taken out of its formal wear and put into some more comfortable clothes. Mathematics should be the life of the party.

Mathematics can be a creative endeavor. Thinking classrooms are creative classrooms. Get kids talking and thinking about fascinating mathematics, and they will show you that mathematics is a creative subject. The range and variety of the student work, the sheer diversity of their thinking, is where creativity is found and celebrated. Subtle divergences in solution paths are seen as we share our solutions. New insights into common problems appear, surprising us.

As teachers, we, too, will be surprised when we see new lines of attack on problems using familiar tools like addition, subtraction, multiplication, and division. Students all will produce their own individual, unique, and interesting representations using drawings or concrete materials. That is what mathematical creativity looks like in problem-solving classrooms.

A misconception about creativity is that it always looks like a sudden bolt from out of the blue, a lightning flash of insight leading to fully formed work being released to the world. "Eureka" moments, as described earlier, are rare. Also rare are the Ramanujans, who seemingly pluck their insights from another world. When Ramanujan arrived at Cambridge to study with Hardy, his notebooks full of proofs astonished. Ramanujan's work was so intensely *different* from the formal proofs preferred by Hardy and other mathematicians. His notebooks were analyzed for many years after his death, mined for their insight and unique approaches to mathematics.

Creative work is more subtle and often appears quietly and unexpectedly. It may just be a variation on the math you expected. It could be a question that arises from a student and spurs him to create more math. Sometimes, only sometimes, it's a lightning flash of insight—an amazing and new solution path that you have never seen before. Creative classrooms are made by valuing student thinking, building mathematical thinkers, and opening up spaces for question-asking as much as question-answering. Watch for more subtle evidence of creativity. Creative mathematical work is there to be found in your classroom.

WE ARE BORN CURIOUS

Humans are born to wonder about many things, including numbers. We are born curious, and we are born to think. We want schools for all children where they are encouraged to play with mathematics.

To be human is to be curious. Leonardo da Vinci is most known for the *Mona Lisa*, but he should be most known for his wide-ranging mind. Above all, he was curious. He took notes about things he wanted to ask about, to get advice about, or just to learn more about. His mind ranged across disciplines, across mathematics, science, art, and engineering. His mind never stopped being curious. Curiosity was his state of being for his entire life. Educators have a chance to make their students curious and capable lifelong learners across the entire range of human endeavors, including mathematics.

Try asking your students this question: *What is something you want to know that can be answered or found out with mathematics?* Give them the sentence stem, "I wonder," and let them wonder. Gather the results on a "wonder wall." Students will ask the most interesting things, and they will wonder things like:

- I wonder if pi ends.
- I wonder how many people have ever lived on this planet.
- I wonder how much money is in the world.

Sort the responses into those that are easily found through an internet search and those that require further investigation. Research where you can. Let wonder be the fuel for mathematics. Let our classrooms be curious places.

We have accepted a state of being where our students are not curious about mathematics at school. At worst, they wait to be given the answers because they know, if they wait long enough, you will give them. If you know any young children, then you probably have noticed they are very curious. They need to know what, why, when, where, and how. If they need to know how to find fossils or how to make a paper airplane, then they *really* need to know and won't be satisfied until they do know. A state of curiosity is an endless state of needing to learn. It is on us, as educators, to make mathematics something students truly, desperately need to know about.

As adults in the working world, it is very possible that our curiosity has become muted even further or that it has completely disappeared. Curiosity goes from something gnawing at our brains, an irresistible desire to learn more, to something that we barely even indulge because we are busy and we just got twenty-two e-mails and our phone just pinged with more notifications. We can, however, regain our sense of wonder. Working with children and listening to them—really listening to them—will do that. Beyond the obvious use and utility of getting through to the end of high school mathematics, we need to graduate students who are still curious about mathematics rather than just blunted by it, bludgeoned by it, and ready to be done with it.

MATHEMATICS IS PLAY (OR AT LEAST IT CAN BE MORE PLAYFUL THAN WE MAKE IT)

Young children know how to play, to learn about the world—they just need our help to make sense of what they are learning. Their worlds are imaginative ones, full of secret spaces and places. Playing to learn is robustly inscribed in kindergarten and early-years curricula and programs, but once kindergarten is over, our students more and more have to leave their imaginative worlds at the schoolhouse door.

School is rules and assignments and bells and endless curriculum standards. You must stop thinking and working when that bell goes off because the bell means "get up and walk down the hall and switch from doing math to doing art." You must produce art on demand. You must produce math when it's time to do math. School life, as the grades progress, becomes more about work than about play.

Play is often seen as a young-child thing. As children get older, the idea of play is frowned upon, and the ethic shifts to work. The amount we play is usually inversely proportional to our age. Adult worlds are less playful still. Adult worlds are full of e-mail and notifications on smartphones and politics and mortgages and taxes and "who's going to pick up the kids from swimming?"

Play is anything you enjoy while you do it. What are the implications for mathematics classrooms? Mathematics classrooms are about work, not play: worksheets, worked examples, bell work, and daily work. They are not usually seen as imaginative spaces, which is a pity because the creation of mathematics is one of the most imaginative leaps ever taken by humans. Mathematics allows us to create other worlds, whole new imaginary worlds. Kids should build "castles" out of mathematics in their minds.

Humans are born playing. We spend our early years learning through play as we learn to move, crawl, walk, and make our way in the world. Play is a basic human desire and, what's more, a basic human *need*. Mathematics can be about play, or at least it can be more playful than we usually make it in our classrooms. Problem-solving classrooms are playful places, where our students engage with interesting mathematics tasks and problems themselves are the very vehicle for learning mathematical ideas and concepts. There is no reason play cannot be part of the daily life of problem-solving classrooms.

Young children play to learn about the world, but educators often discount or forget about the playful mathematical experiences children bring to school with them. Perhaps we are looking for more formal "prior knowledge" about mathematics, and we miss informal or tacit knowledge that we can use in our classrooms. Sometimes we assume that children don't have much in the way of mathematical knowledge and experiences to bring into the classroom.

From birth, though, children learn about shape, quantity, and space by exploring, navigating, and describing the world around them through play. They learn through interacting with puzzles, building a sense of quantity by playing with objects around them, and navigating spatially through their own world. They learn to sort and classify objects, to identify patterns and recognize shapes.

Mathematics is sometimes viewed as esoteric and strange, unnatural, and a secret world that only teachers can give kids access to. We probably do not tend to make the same arguments about literacy. After all, print is abundant in the world around us. We are immersed since birth in text. Perhaps mathematics in the world is harder to find, or maybe we have less experience helping kids to access it. Educators can naturalize mathematical ideas or at least make them seem more natural. This requires seriously intentional talk by early-childhood educators, parents, and teachers, however. Maybe we don't really know how to bring out the math in our world.

With young children, bringing out mathematics can be as simple as asking questions like:

- How many?
- How much?
- How big?
- How long?

We can engage young children in meaningful conversations using specific mathematical-language prompts like these. As young children begin to explore their worlds, they make comparisons, notice when there are more or less objects, and use specific language to compare:

- "There are four more red cars than blue cars."
- "The square is much bigger than the circle."
- "I think there are about twenty blocks."
- "My teacher is as long as two of me."
- "My desk is six pencils wide."
- "I think five of my teacher would be as tall as the school."

Young children play to learn, and teachers can design mathematical experiences that look just like play. Our students are curious, and they can teach us about play. Kids at play are in a deep, deep state of flow. They don't stop playing to eat. They literally forget to eat. They can build Lego worlds and cities for hours. They invent games with their toys and go deep inside the play worlds they have created.

Schools can be against flow, but problem-solving mathematics classrooms can be places where students reach that deep pleasurable state of flow, where the world seems to fade away and we seem to be outside of time. Mathematics can bring us that pleasure, if we provide interesting and worthwhile mathematics tasks and give our students time to talk, think, and wonder.

TOWARD A PEDAGOGY OF PLAYFUL MATHEMATICS

Play is not something that is tangential to learning mathematics. Play should be situated as a necessary component of learning mathematics. We can play to learn the concepts and ideas of mathematics and redefine mathematics as more play than work in our problem-solving classrooms. De Holton, Ahmed, Williams, and Hill (2001) define *mathematical play* as "that part of the process used to solve mathematical problems, which involves both experimentation and creativity to generate ideas, and using the formal rules of mathematics to follow any ideas to some sort of a conclusion." Mathematical play is purposeful play. Teachers have a large role in developing a sense of play in mathematics. As educators, we must be well informed and aware of the various stages and types of play while managing our need to control, direct, and shut it down if it does not serve the intended learning.

As Clements and Sarama (2005) note, "Play does not guarantee mathematical development, but it offers rich possibilities." Teachers as instructional designers set kids to play with intentional learning goals and a roadmap toward a destination of learning about a concept, idea, or skill in mathematics. Mathematical play deserves its own set of axioms, which serves as a subset of our axioms for problem-solving classrooms.

> ### AXIOMS FOR CREATIVE AND PLAYFUL MATHEMATICS CLASSROOMS
>
> 1. Humans are born to play. Play is irrepressibly human.
> 2. We can play to learn. We can play with mathematics to learn mathematics.
> 3. Mathematical ideas are meant to be played with.
> 4. Playing and thinking are not at odds with each other. A playing state can be a thinking state.
> 5. Mathematics is full of surprises. Surprises are pleasurable.
> 6. A pedagogy of playful mathematics is a pedagogy of hopeful mathematics. All mathematics classrooms should be playful classrooms, where teachers guide kids through carefully designed experiences of ideas and concepts in mathematics.
> 7. Thinking and problem-solving are messy, playful, and fun. Embrace the mess of the problem-solving process; listen and talk to your students as they work.
> 8. Mathematics is a creative, generative process.

Mathematical play builds virtues that enable us to flourish in every area of our lives. For instance, math play builds hopefulness: when you sit with a puzzle long enough, you are exercising hope that you will eventually solve it. Math play builds community when you share in the delight of working on a problem with another human being. Math play builds perseverance; just as weekly soccer practices build the muscles that make us stronger for the next game, math investigations make us more fit for the next problem, whatever that is, even if we don't solve the current problem.

Play builds hope, as Francis Su says, in his aforementioned talk "Mathematics for Human Flourishing." Play, pure and unrefined, is an expression of freedom; it is every person's right, especially a child's. If we define *math* as play, then math builds hope. Math play builds hope. Mathematics builds hope in children, or at least, it can. As I have already mentioned, Su tells of a prisoner who, learning mathematics, escapes, if not time, then at least his space of physical confinement, by learning mathematics. Mathematics for him was a signifier of hope for the future.

Mathematics Can Be Playful

A pedagogy of playful mathematics is a pedagogy of hopeful mathematics. All mathematics classrooms should be playful classrooms. Dr. Cathy Bruce envisions a playful pedagogy as a kind of guided play for children, with teachers guiding kids through powerful and big ideas in mathematics. Let it be so! Pure play, or play with no set goal, can be distinguished from classroom mathematical play.

Teachers are accountable to curriculum, so mathematical play in our classrooms is often goal oriented. We might deploy a deck of cards to practice adding and subtracting integers, for example, or use dice games to practice order of operations. Games can also serve as problems themselves to explore and experience mathematical ideas. Consider this example:

> Roll 10 identical six-sided dice. How often will you come up with four of a kind?

In this case, the game play itself allows students to bring the theoretical probability into the world through experimentation.

You flip a coin ten times. Is it reasonable that your outcome looks like this?

> HTHTHTHTHT

Students should flip coins many times to see what is happening with this probability. Pure randomness does not really exist. A straight alternation between heads and tails is unlikely. Better yet, have students flip a coin fifty times and record the results in a string like shown. Now have them, right below that string, make up a fake string of fifty coin flips. It is very likely they will overemphasize the alternation of heads and tails, or the "fifty-fifty-ness," whereas real-life coin flipping will see longer strings, like, for example, "HHHHH" within any given longer string.

Gamification of problems builds engagement, and games can be used in service of mathematical thinking. It has been said that play is the highest form of learning. A pedagogy of playful mathematics might even be the highest form of mathematics pedagogy. Kindergarten teachers in play-based programs are highly trained at helping kids learn through play. Play, in general, drops off as kids go through the grades. What if we played more with our mathematics in every grade?

Science gets all the hands-on love in schools. Kids get to learn science by playing, doing, and touching. They can fly paper airplanes to learn about flight. They can mix oil and water to see what happens. Mathematical ideas need more hands-on love. Play with dice to learn about chance. Tape a giant number line all along your classroom floor, and have your students stand on it to represent fractions. Illustrate integer subtraction by taking steps forward and backward. Fill containers with water to show how fractions relate to a whole.

Mathematical ideas need to be translated from the perfect world in which they live into our world. Mathematical objects shouldn't sit on dusty shelves. They are meant to be brought to life and to be played with. If your imagination is big enough, you can do mathematics. Remember Max, in his "wild rumpus," using his imagination to travel beyond his physical boundaries. We all have big imaginations; we just don't use them enough. We want a "no-limits mathematics," one that is bounded only by our imaginations.

ALL STUDENTS SHOULD PLAY WITH BIG AND POWERFUL MATHEMATICAL IDEAS

All children should play with big and powerful mathematical ideas. Let your students play with the big and powerful ideas and tools of mathematics, and let them surprise you with the power of their thinking.

The Case of Infinity

Have you ever asked a very young child, "What's the biggest number you know?" When they are little, they might say, "Ten." Then they learn to do a bit of arithmetic or to count higher, and they might say, "One hundred." But try this: Add one each time. Whatever number they give you, add one.

You might hear a conversation like this between two five-year-olds:

"How high can you count?"
"I can count to infinity!"
"Oh, yeah? I can count to infinity plus one!"

Variations of this conversation have been played out countless times over the years. If humans exist for an infinite number of years more, then this conversation will happen an infinite number of times. Young minds are perfectly tuned to think about infinity. They don't need Cantor sets and elaborate proofs of the infinite number of primes to play to consider the largeness of infinity. We are born to wonder about infinity, and yet, where is it in kindergarten to grade 12 curricula? It is barely there, if at all.

One powerful memory I have is my son, perhaps age four, emptying his piggy bank and saying, "I have infinity money. I have more than I can count." How did he even know the word *infinity*? How is it that a four-year-old could come up with such a great definition of *infinity*?

Try using this statement in your classroom and see where the conversation goes:

Infinity is a number you can never reach, no matter how high you count.

Ask for a definition from your students, regardless of what grade you teach. Chances are, they will have some idea about infinity and want to share it with you. They cannot use the tools that professional mathematicians use to tame infinity, but they can imagine infinity. Imagination has no limits.

The Other Half of the Number Line

Another idea that is typically hidden until later is the other half of the natural number line—the negative half. But if children are taught to count forward, then can they not also be taught to count backward? What happens when you reach zero? A child might say something like, "You can't go below zero." It seems natural that numbers would stop at zero; after all, they are taught since birth to count in the other direction. Even rocket blastoff countdowns end at zero.

This did happen. "Three subtract seven is zero," my six-year-old son said. He ate the three M&Ms we were using as counters for our subtraction practice. Consuming all the food in front of us is a powerful representation of zero.

"There's nothing left. I could only take away three." Children are usually taught to think of subtraction first as "taking away." He took away the three M&Ms that we had, and there was nothing left. What to do? Let his current understanding stand, or push him into the new and surprising world of negative numbers?

It is easy to underestimate a young child's nascent mathematical understanding. It would be easy to leave this problem alone for now because negative integers are, some might say, beyond his current understanding. We did not leave it alone. We had a chance to open up a new mathematical frontier.

What happens when you try to take a bigger number away from a smaller number? Adults have internalized the idea that every positive integer has its opposite, an equal distance from zero on the negative side of the number line. Most of us, at least if we live where the Celsius scale is used for temperature, have at least some comfort with these "imaginary" numbers.

Subtraction is typically shown to students in grade 1 as an operation of taking away or removal, but subtraction falls apart or breaks at zero using this instantiation of subtraction. We reached the "zero M&M barrier." There is nothing less than zero M&Ms. A negative M&M, or "anti-M&M" cannot possibly exist. Our options were either to stop there or to develop a new conceptual tool for thinking about this problem.

You can forgive students for thinking, as they progress through the grades in mathematics, that they are being introduced to new kinds of numbers that appear like magic at a teacher's command: there are fractions, which appear as an entirely new form that are mysteriously different from the counting numbers, and there are integers (or rather their negative half), which appear around the age of eleven in most curricula.

"Can you keep counting below zero?" I asked.

"No."

Counting is complexity disguised as simplicity. Kids love to count; they are just trained to only count in one direction. Although counting seems natural, kids progress through a lot of steps as they learn to count. They probably begin with rote repetition of the counting sequence. They learn one-to-one tagging, where one finger points to one object at a time, and conservation of number. The big move they make next is using the familiar Arabic digits to represent numbers. Thinking about negative numbers is a bigger abstraction but one of which they are more than capable.

We took out more M&Ms. "Show me eight subtract four."

"Eight subtract four is four."

This was no problem. He just counted backward and removed the M&Ms.

We modeled more subtraction expressions with our candy counters. "Ten subtract five is five."

"Five subtract five is zero." Now, that mysterious hinge point, zero, appeared. We would either open new mathematical ground or stop here.

"Three subtract seven is zero."

Zero is itself strange, a conception of nothingness that jars with the way kids are taught counting, adding, and subtracting by working with concrete objects. We perhaps do not naturally think about emptiness or nothingness. "Nothing will come of nothing," as Shakespeare said. If there are not objects on the table in front of us, then we do not necessarily need a name to tell us that. Humans did not invent zero for mathematical purposes for many thousands of years, but when we needed it to show the erasure of debt, sure enough, we conjured it into being.

We drew a number line. *Difference*, on a number line, is an understanding of subtraction that usually comes along later, after *taking away*. I marked zero, one, two, three, leaving zero as the very left-hand edge of the number line.

Talking mathematics with small children sometimes means inventing new mathematics right in front of our eyes. We needed to count below zero, so we figured out how to do it. We needed the concept of negative integers to solve his problem. The big teaching moment had arrived. He just needed prompting to start counting: "minus one, minus two," and so on. This was the moment where I would make it seem natural, as if those negative numbers just had to be there.

"Can you count below zero?"

"No."

"How do they tell you the temperature in winter?"

He thought about it for a while and then said, "Minus five."

We sketched jumps backward from three on the number line: two, one, zero.

"Is minus one next?"

"Yes."

We jumped from zero to minus one, to minus two, to minus three, and to minus four. The other half of the number line suddenly came into being.

"What is three subtract seven?"

"Minus four!"

Children are capable and curious. They don't need to be sheltered from big mathematical ideas. Bring out mathematical ideas when kids are ready or when they are needed. Mathematics learning is developmental, and we can help them with their development. We opened up an entire new world of counting, where you can count forward and backward from zero whenever you want. My son used his newfound mathematical power to start counting in a new way.

"Minus one, minus two, minus three, minus four."

There is a tendency on the part of teachers to hide mathematical concepts from young children because they aren't ready. This is, in part, a natural response to the grueling demands of curriculum; there is a lockstep progression through the content standards from grade to grade. The grade 3 teacher does not want to disrupt the grade 4 teacher by teaching ahead. Students must do their careful apprenticeship from learning to count to learning advanced algebra and calculus in their kindergarten to grade 12 mathematics education because that is what has always been done.

There are mathematical ideas so massive that we might assume children cannot handle them. But mathematics belongs to the imagination, and children have massive, world-spanning imaginations. We should talk about infinity with three-year-olds. Five-year-olds should twist doughnuts into tori to explore basic ideas of topology. Eight-year-olds should break apart the standard multiplication algorithm to see how it works. Nine-year-olds should break apart numbers into their atomic prime bits and put them back together again. And yes, the big ideas of calculus can be shown to young children. Quantities change over time at different rates of speed. Even funny and strange shapes can be divided into rectangles. Tell me children wouldn't love playing with that idea.

Our problem-solving pedagogy is a playful one, taking as the objects of play all the interesting mathematics we can handle. Teachers are the guides to big ideas in mathematics, guiding students through playful and, dare we say it, fun experiences. A playful problem-solving pedagogy takes for granted that we are only limited by our imaginations, which are endless like oceans seem to be but, unlike oceans, have no boundaries.

Coda

QED?

Teaching is aspirational work. If we, as educators, did not believe that we can help our students to learn important facts and ideas about the world and, in turn, to learn about themselves as learners and as thinking humans making their way in the world, then we would probably give up and find another, less stressful line of work. Teaching is reflective work: teach, reflect, improve, repeat. All teachers of mathematics aspire to having students who are knowledgeable about mathematics, using their skills, tools, and reasoning as they think their way through challenging tasks and problems.

Problems can and should be the vehicle for learning mathematics. Problems are at the heart of mathematics itself. Problem-solving classrooms are thinking classrooms, big, wide, open, unbounded mental spaces for thinking about problematic mathematics tasks and questions and for bringing that mathematics into being. This "bringing into being" is the entire mental process of developing a mental representation of a problem and finding a way to bring it from the world of thought into the world of matter and objects. This is done by writing, drawing, and speaking and by physically manipulating objects. Students, as novices, are guided through seeing the power of their representations and seeing their representations as valuable expressions of their mathematical thinking.

Problem-solving classrooms are aspirational, and they are inspirational. Our goal is, only in part, to help students get through all their math courses to the end of high school. We have a bigger, broader, more human goal: to show students the pleasure and power of thinking mathematically as they build their tool kit of skills and engage with the massive and astonishing ideas of mathematics. Mathematics classrooms should surprise students with the beauty, power, and subtlety of mathematics on a daily basis.

There exists a mathematics education that builds mathematical thinkers who are as adept with concepts as they are with basic skills and leaves them in a forever curious state, wanting, not needing, to learn more mathematics. No more "I hated math in school." No more "I was just never any good at math." As educators, it is our job to conjure this school mathematics into being. The systemic barriers (outmoded or constantly changing curriculum documents, established ways of doing things, college and university prerequisites) will not stand in our way.

Mathematics, the discipline, with all its attendant notation, big ideas, facts, and seemingly esoteric power, is far different from school mathematics, and yet, the intersection of the two is where our students learn. There exists a Venn diagram showing the intersection of "all mathematics" and "school mathematics." Mathematics itself could be said to be the study of structure; the science of patterns; the science of number, quantity, and space; or the systematic and scientific study of structure. Our classrooms are places where mathematics comes to life, where hidden structures are revealed, where patterns are taken apart into their basic elements, and where we learn big ideas about number and shapes.

Many of the advanced actions, theorems, and conjectures of pure and applied mathematics do not apply to school mathematics, and yet, our novices, our learners, learn to think mathematically and to use interesting problems and tasks to learn skills and concepts. Our students reason with numbers; represent mathematics through their thoughts, verbally, and on paper; prove their results to themselves and others; and communicate their thinking to classmates and teachers. Students think about mathematics, talk about mathematics, and represent mathematics in problem-solving classrooms. That this school mathematics to which we aspire be brought into being is a matter of great urgency. Teachers have an immense power to influence how their students perceive mathematics *itself*.

Having read this book, now consider what would happen if you went to school tomorrow and asked your students this question: *What is mathematics?* Would you be pleased with their answers? Or disappointed at their internalized narrow viewpoint based on their experiences with school mathematics? Try it, and see what happens.

If the school year started tomorrow, then what problem would you give to get your students thinking? A first-day problem can open up the classroom as a big, wide field for thinking. Rules, regulations, and review can wait until the next day. Engage with a problem on the first day of class.

Me, I might just ask them, What would happen if octopuses learned to count? What would that look like?

Or I might ask them a problem we have already discussed: Would you want me to give you a penny that doubles each day for a month or $1,000,000 right now?

Or a related and more ancient version of this problem: If you put one grain of sand on the first square of a chessboard and then doubled that grain for each subsequent square (1, 2, 4, 8 . . .), then how many grains of sand would it take to fill the chessboard?

How long would it take to count to a million?

How many of you would you have to lay down to create the perimeter of the soccer field?

Maybe you could just ask, Why are 25, 36, and 64 interesting numbers? Is 225 the same type of interesting number? How do you know?

Play with 9 × 9. Break it apart.

Why can't you break 83 or 89 apart?

How would you calculate 492 divided by 24 without a calculator?

Why is 0 important?

How big is infinity?

How many little centimeter cubes would fill this classroom? Is it in the thousands? Millions? Billions?

How many liters or gallons of water would fill this classroom?

And so on, we could go. Open your classroom doors wide, and invite students to think. Create a living and vibrant culture of mathematical discourse. Think, reason, conjecture, and wonder. Play.

Many students, before they enter your classroom, might describe math as something they don't like but is necessary, like broccoli or cough medicine or booster shots. After they leave your classroom for the last time, how will they describe mathematics?

Remember, to many of our students, mathematics *is* the narrow set of worksheets, procedures, and formulae that we give them. That is the way it is, but it is your job to change their way of thinking. It is your job to guide them along the way, to mentor their thinking as young mathematicians.

I have made the case for our students as mathematical, capable thinkers; as problem-solvers; and as bringers into being of powerful mathematics. For the record, here are a few anonymous responses to the sentence starter "Math is" from students of various ages who learned mathematics in a problem-solving environment:

SOME THINGS STUDENTS HAVE SAID IN RESPONSE TO THE PROMPT "MATH IS"

The language to explain certain happenings.

> Fun for me. Math is all around us.
> I love to do math because, first, it makes your mind smarter. Next, it just makes me happy.
> Important, since, well, it's used everywhere for everything, and so it's basically necessary in our lives.
> Everywhere.
> A way of solving equations/problems. Math is everything, everything is math.
> A combination of numbers and symbols that is useful for everyday life and can help you in the future.

One sixth-grade philosopher said this:

> Math is everything. Everywhere you go, everyone you meet, all have some connection with math. It's logic, common sense, and thinking out of the box, not only the seemingly tedious arithmetic and problem-solving. Math has grown into the world, and so the world wouldn't be the world without it.

An eighth-grade student profoundly said of mathematics,

> It's a metaphor of life. It asks you to solve the problems it creates. It's simple. It's just us creating ways to explain things we don't fully understand.

I dream of a school mathematics where kids in classrooms around the world learn by engaging daily with problems, and if we can dream of it, then we can bring it into being. Mathematics is an act of creation. Teaching is an act of creation; teachers help students to gain knowledge, to develop their understanding of ideas, and to apply concepts and skills. Teaching is "making new," a creative activity where teachers design courses of study that are engaging and accountable to curriculum standards, the discipline of mathematics, and the culture of the classroom.

Together, let us bring into being a school mathematics that graduates students who are confident mathematical thinkers. Let us bring into being a school mathematics that makes kids confident problem-solvers who can use the tools and ideas of mathematics. Let us bring into being a school mathematics that builds creative and critical thinking using the tools of mathematics.

Together, let us bring into being a school mathematics that is beautiful, elegant, and true.

Let us bring into being a school mathematics that is rigorous and formal yet playful.

Let us bring into being a school mathematics where students play with numbers, shapes, and other things.

Let us bring into being a school mathematics where students learn to think mathematically, stripping problems confidently down to their essentials and putting forth self-assured and persuasive solutions.

Let us bring into being a school mathematics where mathematical ideas are talked about, examined, discussed, and played with.

Let us build a school mathematics that leaves kids begging for more; going home at night to think about compelling tasks and problems; and coming back to school the next day with fresh energy, insights, and ideas.

We need to treat this as a matter of some urgency, so let's think it, write it, and talk it into being. Mathematics deserves no less, and more importantly, our students deserve no less. The last word, as always, must go to a student. If we trust in their thinking, then we will be rewarded. They are the reason we show up in the classroom every single day.

A student once said:

> Mathematics is the most powerful force in the universe. Use it wisely.

So we must.

Bibliography

Bennett, Sheila, Don Dworet, and K. J. Weber. 2008. *Special Education in Ontario Schools*. Niagara-on-the-Lake, ON: Highland Press.

Black, Paul, and Dylan William. 1998. "Inside the Black Box: Raising Standards through Classroom Assessment." *Phi Delta Kappan* 80, no. 2: 139–48.

Bruce, Catherine D. 2007. "Student Interaction in the Math Classroom: Stealing Ideas or Building Understanding." *Literacy and Numeracy Secretariat*. January. http://www.edu.gov.on.ca/eng/literacynumeracy/inspire/research/Bruce.pdf (accessed February 24, 2018).

Cai, Jinfa, and Frank Lester. 2010. "Why Is Teaching through Problem Solving Important to Student Learning?" *National Council of Teachers of Mathematics*. April 8. https://www.nctm.org/uploadedFiles/Research_and_Advocacy/research_brief_and_clips/Research_brief_14_-_Problem_Solving.pdf (accessed 2014).

Clements, Douglas H., and Julie Sarama. 2005. "Math Play: How Young Children Approach Math." *Scholastic Early Childhood Today* (January/February): 50–57.

Common Core State Standards Initiative. 2015. *Common Core State Standards for Mathematics*. http://www.corestandards.org/wp-content/uploads/Math_Standards1.pdf (accessed February 24, 2018).

De Holton, Derek, Afzal Ahmed, Honor Williams, and Christine Hill. 2001. "On the Importance of Mathematical Play." *International Journal of Mathematical Education in Science and Technology* 32, no. 3: 401–415.

Devlin, Keith. 2012. "What *Is* Mathematical Thinking?" *Devlin's Angle*. September 1. http://devlinsangle.blogspot.ca/2012/08/what-is-mathematical-thinking.html (accessed 2014).

Dickinson, Emily. 2000. *The Complete Poems of Emily Dickinson*. Boston: Little, Brown; Bartleby.com. www.bartleby.com/113/ (accessed July 10, 2018).

Ellenberg, Jordan. 2014. *How Not To Be Wrong: The Power of Mathematical Thinking*. New York: The Penguin Press.

Fullan, Michael. 2013. "The New Pedagogy: Teachers and Students as Learning Partners." *LEARNing Landscapes* 6, no. 2 (Spring): 23–29. https://michaelfullan.ca/wp-content/uploads/2013/08/Commentary-Learning-Landscapes-New-Pedagogy.pdf (accessed February 24, 2018).

Hattie, John, Douglas Fisher, and Nancy Frey. 2017. *Visible Learning for Mathematics*. Thousand Oaks, CA: Corwin Mathematics.

Kirschner, Paul, John Sweller, and Richard E. Clark. 2006. "Why Minimal Guidance during Instruction Does Not Work: An Analysis of the Failure of Constructivist, Discovery, Problem-Based, Experiential, and Inquiry-Based Teaching." *Educational Psychologist* 41, no. 2: 75–86.

Lappan, Glenda, and Diane Briars. 1995. "How Should Mathematics Be Taught?" In *Seventy-Five Years of Progress: Prospects for School Mathematics*, edited by Iris M. Carl, pp. 131–56. Reston, VA: National Council of Teachers of Mathematics.

Liljedahl, Peter. 2016. "Building Thinking Classrooms: Conditions for Problem Solving." In *Posing and Solving Mathematical Problems: Advances and New Perspectives*, edited by P. Felmer, J. Kilpatrick, and E. Pekhonen, 361–86. New York: Springer. http://www.peterliljedahl.com/wp-content/uploads/Building-Thinking-Classrooms-Feb-14-2015.pdf (accessed February 1, 2018).

Lockhart, Paul. 2002. "A Mathematician's Lament." *Mathematical Association of America*. https://www.maa.org/external_archive/devlin/LockhartsLament.pdf (accessed 2014).

Marzano, Robert J. 2010. "What Teachers Gain from Deliberate Practice." *Educational Leadership* 68, no. 4: 82–85.

Meyer, Dan. 2018. "Duelling Discounts." Blog. MrMeyer.Com. http://threeacts.mrmeyer.com/duelingdiscounts/ (accessed July 10, 2018).

National Council of Teachers of Mathematics. 2000. *Principles and Standards for School Mathematics*. Reston, VA: National Council of Teachers of Mathematics.

Pape, Stephen, and Mourat Tchoshanov. 2001. "The Role of Representation(s) in Developing Mathematical Understanding." *Theory into Practice* 40, no. 2: 118–27.

Piggott, Jennifer. 2008. "Rich Tasks and Contexts." *NRICH*. September. https://nrich.maths.org/5662/index (accessed 2014).

Pink, Daniel H. 2009. *Drive: The Surprising Truth About What Motivates Us*. New York: Riverhead Books.

Polya, Georg. 2014. *How to Solve It: A New Aspect of Mathematical Method*. Princeton, NJ: Princeton University Press.

Ontario Ministry of Education. 2005. *The Ontario Curriculum: Mathematics, Grades 1–8: Mathematics*. http://www.edu.gov.on.ca/eng/curriculum/elementary/math18curr.pdf (accessed February 24, 2018).

Rittle-Johnson, Bethany, Robert S. Siegler, and Martha Wagner Alibali. 2001. "Developing Conceptual Understanding and Procedural Skill in Mathematics: An Iterative Process." *Journal of Educational Psychology* 93, no. 2: 346–62.

Schoenfeld, Alan H. 1992. "Learning to Think Mathematically: Problem Solving, Metacognition, and Sense Making in Mathematics." In *Handbook for Research on Mathematics Teaching and Learning*, edited by D. Grouws, 355–58. New York: Macmillan.

Stefanakis, Evangeline. 2002. *Multiple Intelligences and Portfolios*. Portsmouth, NH: Heinemann.

Su, Francis. 2017. "Mathematics For Human Flourishing." *The Mathematical Yawp*. https://mathyawp.wordpress.com/2017/01/08/mathematics-for-human-flourishing/ (accessed July 10, 2018).

Van de Walle, John. 2004. *Elementary and Middle School Mathematics: Teaching Developmentally*. New York: Allyn and Bacon.

Wieman, Robert, and Fran Arbaugh. 2013. *Success from the Start: Your First Years Teaching Secondary Mathematics*. Reston, VA: National Council of Teachers of Mathematics.

Wiggins, Grant. 2014. "Conceptual Understanding in Mathematics." *Granted and . . . :Thoughts on Education by Grant Wiggins*. April 23.https://grantwiggins.wordpress.com/2014/04/23/conceptual-understanding-in-mathematics (accessed 2015).

Wiggins, G., and J. McTighe. 1998. *Understanding by Design*. Alexandria, VA: Association for Supervision and Curriculum Development.

Willingham, Daniel. 2009–2010. "Is It True That Some People Just Can't Do Math?" *American Educator* (Winter 2009-2010): 14–19, 39. https://www.aft.org/sites/default/files/periodicals/willingham.pdf (accessed February 24, 2018).

Index

aesthetics of Art, 20–21
aesthetics of mathematics, 21–22
assessment, 83, 85–87

beauty, 4, 5, 20
Bruce, Dr. Cathy, 81, 101

Cheng, Dr. Eugenia, 10
cognitive load, 14, 26
collaboration, 78, 81
contexts, real-world, 6, 7, 9
creative thinking, 93–94, 95–96
critical thinking, 89–90
counting, 42, 51, 104
creation, 45
creativity, xii
curiosity, 96–97

da Vinci, Leonardo, and creativity, 96
Devlin, Keith, 28
Dickinson, Emily, xi
direct instruction, 14–15, 65, 70
discourse in mathematics classrooms, 78, 79, 80, 82

Erdos, Paul, 21
Ellenberg, Jordan, xii, 23
existential quantifier, xiii

feedback, 84
fractions, 4–5, 42, 55, 84

Frobenius numbers, 15

Gauss, Carl Friedrich, 25, 28

heuristics, 33, 36–37, 38
How to Solve It, 33–34

infinity, xi, 102–103
inquiry, 8, 63–64
instructional guidance, 66–67, 70
integers, 71–72, 103

keywords, 26
knowledge, 50, 53

Lockhart, Paul, 29
Liljedahl, Peter, 20
literacy, 24

mathematical thinking, xiii, 19, 22–23, 25, 26, 28–30, 31, 36
mathematizing, 8
math wars, xv
Melville, Herman, 24
memorization, 52–53
metacognition, 40, 41
Meyer, Dan, 80
multiplication, 11–13, 25, 43, 47–50, 53, 58

NCTM standards, 44, 61, 90

115

novice vs. expert, 30–31, 38
numbers, 24, 25

pedagogy, 10, 61–62
pedagogy, of playful mathematics, 99–101, 105
pi, 68–69
play, xiii, 97–98, 99–101
Polya, Georg, 33
practice, 71–72, 73
problem (definition), 3, 4, 5
problem-solving, xii, 2–3, 11, 30, 34
problem-solving, skills and strategies, 39–40
problem-solving, teaching about, 2
problem-solving, teaching through, 2, 14
procedural vs. conceptual understanding, 54, 56–57, 58–59, 73
prime numbers, 25
Pythagorean Theorem, 4, 11–12, 13, 57

Ramanujan, 25, 95
reasoning, xiii, 88, 91

representations, 23, 34, 38, 41, 42, 44, 45, 50
rich tasks, 13

standard algorithms, 47–48
Su, Francis, xiii, 100

teaching through problem-solving-definition, 13
tests, 84–85, 87
thinking, xii, 5, 20
thinking tools, 27

understanding, 51–52, 53–54
unit rates, 3

visualizing, xii

Wiggins, Grant, 53
Wiles, Andrew, 16
Where the Wild Things Are, 10
Willingham, Daniel, 59
word problems, 5, 6
worksheets, xiii, 5, 77–78

About the Author

Matthew Oldridge is a father, husband, mathematics educator, two-time TEDx speaker ("Math Is Play" and "Math Classrooms Should Be Full of Surprise and Wonder"), and general "thinker about things." He has taught or facilitated mathematics for more than sixteen years to students, kindergarten to grade 12, as a classroom teacher and mathematics consultant.

His thoughts and opinions about mathematics education, books, ideas, and world issues appear on his Twitter feed, @MatthewOldridge, and on Medium. He has written and appeared in video projects for the Ontario Ministry of Education; in the *Globe and Mail*; and coast to coast on Canada's national broadcaster, CBC radio.

Please join the conversation by contacting him through Twitter or his website, www.matthewoldridge.com.

CPSIA information can be obtained
at www.ICGtesting.com
Printed in the USA
LVHW041512140219
607562LV00010B/116/P